Lecture Notes in Computer Science 8425

Commenced Publication in 1973
Founding and Former Series Editors:
Gerhard Goos, Juris Hartmanis, and Jan van Leeuwen

For further volumes:
http://www.springer.com/series/7409

Willem Jonker · Milan Petković (Eds.)

Secure
Data Management

10th VLDB Workshop, SDM 2013
Trento, Italy, August 30, 2013
Proceedings

Springer

Editors

Willem Jonker
EIT ICT Labs/University of Twente
Enschede
The Netherlands

Milan Petković
Philips Research/Eindhoven University
   of Technology
Eindhoven
The Netherlands

ISSN 0302-9743   ISSN 1611-3349 (electronic)
ISBN 978-3-319-06810-7   ISBN 978-3-319-06811-4 (eBook)
DOI 10.1007/978-3-319-06811-4
Springer Cham Heidelberg New York Dordrecht London

Library of Congress Control Number: 2014938481

LNCS Sublibrary: SL3 – Information Systems and Applications, incl. Internet/Web, and HCI

Printed on acid-free paper

Springer is part of Springer Science+Business Media (www.springer.com)

Preface

The 2013 VLDB Secure Data Management Workshop was the tenth edition of the SDM workshop series.

Recent developments in society have led to a growing interest in the topic of data security. The deep embedding of ICT in our everyday life has resulted in an ever-growing amount of (often personal) data traveling over the World Wide Web. Awareness of the need for proper protection of these data is growing among citizens, industries, and politicians.

Given the fact that the tenth edition of our VLDB Secure Data Management Workshop was an anniversary edition, we decided to hold a special workshop with a proceedings volume comprising the visionary contributions of leading thinkers in the field.

The result of the workshop is captured in these proceedings, which contain the keynote paper, the technical papers, as well as ten vision papers. The vision papers in particular address key challenges in our area and indicate interesting research questions. We hope that these vision papers will inspire researchers in this field and give direction to their research.

We wish to thank all the authors of submitted papers for their high-quality submissions. We would also like to thank the Program Committee members as well as the additional reviewers for doing an excellent job. Finally, we would like to acknowledge Elisa Costante and Sokratis Vavilis, who helped in the technical preparation of the proceedings.

December 2013

Willem Jonker
Milan Petković

Organization

Workshop Organizers

Willem Jonker   EIT ICT Labs/University of Twente, Enschede,
The Netherlands

Milan Petković   Philips Research/Eindhoven University of
Technology, Eindhoven, The Netherlands

Program Committee

Gerrit Bleumer
Ljiljana Brankovic
Sabrina De Capitani di Vimercati
Ernesto Damiani
Eric Diehl
Jeroen Doumen
Csilla Farkas
Eduardo Fernández-Medina
Elena Ferrari
Simone Fischer-Hubner
Tyrone Grandison
Dieter Gollmann
Hakan Hacigumus
Marit Hansen
Min-Shiang Hwang
Mizuho Iwaihara
Sushil Jajodia
Ton Kalker
Marc Langheinrich

Nguyen Manh Tho
Nick Mankovich
Sharad Mehrotra
Stig Frode Mjolsnes
Eiji Okamoto
Sylvia Osborn
Guenther Pernul
Birgit Pfitzmann
Bart Preneel
Kai Rannenberg
David G. Rosado
Ahmad-Reza Sadeghi
Andreas Schaad
Jason Smith
Morton Swimmer
Clark Thomborson
Sheng Zhong
Nicola Zannone

Organization

Contents

Key Note

To Cloud Or Not To?
Musings on Clouds, Security and Big Data

Radu Sion(✉)

Stony Brook Network Security and Applied Cryptography Lab,
Stony Brook, USA
radu@digitalpiglet.org

Abstract. In this talk we explored the economics of cloud computing. We identified cost trade-offs and postulated the key principles of cloud outsourcing that define when cloud deployment is appropriate and why. The results may surprise and are especially interesting in understanding cyber- security aspects that impact the appeal of clouds.

We outlined and investigated some of the main research challenges on optimizing for these trade-offs. If you came to this talk you were also very likely to find out exactly how many US dollars you need to spend to break your favorite cipher, or send one of your bits over the network.

1 Overview

Commoditized outsourced computing has finally arrived, mainly due to the emergence of fast and cheap networking and efficient large scale computing. Amazon, Google, Microsoft and Oracle are just a few of the providers starting to offer increasingly complex storage and computation outsourcing "cloud" services. CPU cycles have become consumer merchandise.

In [1] and elsewhere we explored the end-to-end cost of a CPU cycle in various environments and show that its cost lies between 0.45 picocents in efficient clouds and 27 picocents for small business deployment scenarios (1 picocent $= \$1 \times 10^{-14}$). In terms of pure CPU cycle costs, current clouds present seemingly cost-effective propositions for personal and small enterprise clients.

Nevertheless, cloud clients are concerned with the **privacy of their data and computation** – this is often the primary adoption obstacle, especially for medium and large corporations, who often fall under strict regulatory compliance requirements. To address this, existing secure outsourcing research addressed several issues including guaranteeing integrity, confidentiality and privacy of outsourced data to secure querying on outsourced encrypted database. Such assurances will likely require strong cryptography as part of elaborate intra- and client-cloud protocols. Yet, strong crypto is expensive. Thus, it is important to ask: how much cryptography can we afford in the cloud while maintaining the cost benefits of outsourcing?

Some believe the answer is simply *none*. In a 2009 interview, Whitfield Diffie argued that "the whole point of cloud computing is economy" and while it is

W. Jonker and M. Petković (Eds.): SDM 2013, LNCS 8425, pp. 3–5, 2014.
DOI: 10.1007/978-3-319-06811-4_1, © Springer International Publishing Switzerland 2014

possible in principle for "computation to be done on encrypted data, [...] *current techniques would more than undo the economy gained by the outsourcing and show little sign of becoming practical*".

In this work we explored whether this is truly the case. We set out to find out whether this holds and if so, by what margins. We would like to quantify just *how* expensive it is to secure computing in untrusted, potentially curious clouds.

One way to look at this is in terms of CPU cycles. For each desired unsecured client CPU cycle, *how many additional cloud cycles can we spend on cryptography*, before its outsourcing becomes too expensive?

We started by looking at the economics of computing in general and clouds in particular. Specifically, we derived the end-to-end cost of a CPU cycle in various environments and show that its cost lies between 0.1 picocents in efficient clouds and nearly 27 picocents for small enterprises (1 picocent $= \$1 \times 10^{-14}$), values *validated against current cloud pricing*.

We then explored the cost of common cryptography primitives as well as the viability of their deployment for cloud security purposes. We conclude that Diffie was correct. Securing outsourced data and computation against untrusted clouds is indeed costlier than the associated savings, with outsourcing mechanisms up to several orders of magnitudes costlier than their non-outsourced locally run alternatives.

This is simply because today's cryptography does not allow for *efficient* oblivious processing of *complex enough* functions on encrypted data. And outsourcing simple operations – such as existing research in querying encrypted data, keyword searches, selections, projections, and simple aggregates – is simply not profitable (too few compute cycles / input word to offset the client's distance from the cloud). Thus, while traditional security mechanisms allow the elegant handling of inter-client and outside adversaries, today it is still too costly to secure against cloud insiders with cryptography.

2   Conclusion

In this work we explored whether cryptography can be deployed to secure cloud computing against insiders. In the process we evaluated CPU cycles at a price of no less than 0.1 picocents, and saw that a bit cannot be transferred without paying at least 900 picocents, and stored a year without a pocket setback of at least 100 picocents. We estimated common cryptography costs (AES, MD5, SHA-1, RSA, DSA, and ECDSA) and finally explored outsourcing of data and computation to untrusted clouds. We showed that deploying the cloud as a simple remote encrypted file system is extremely unfeasible if considering only core technology costs. Similarly, existing single server cryptographic oblivious data access protocols are not only time-impractical (this has been shown previously) but also (surprisingly) orders of magnitude more dollar expensive than trivial data transfer. We also concluded that existing secure outsourced data query mechanisms are mostly cost-unfeasible because **today's cryptography simply lacks the**

expressive power to efficiently support computation outsourcing to untrusted clouds. Hope is not lost however. Full homomorphisms are becoming increasingly faster. Further, for simple data outsourcing, we found borderline cases where outsourcing of simple range queries can break even when compared with local execution. These scenarios involve large amounts of outsourced data (e.g., 10^9 tuples) and extremely selective queries which return only an infinitesimal fraction of the original data (e.g., 0.00037 %).

The scope did not permit us to explore the fascinating broader issues at the intersection of technology with business models, risk, behavioral incentives, socio-economics, and advertising markets. We also would have liked to explore how "green" factors impact computing or whether mobile power and computation-constrained scenarios would be different.

About the Author

Radu is an Associate Professor of Computer Science at Stony Brook University (on leave) and currently the CEO of Private Machines Inc., an early startup funded by the US Air Force, OSD, IARPA, the National Science Foundation and others. He remembers when gophers were digging through the Internets and bits were running at slower paces of 512 per second. He is also interested in efficient computing with a touch of cyber-security paranoia, raising rabbits on space ships and sailing catamarans of the Hobie variety. Radu lives in Brooklyn, NY.

Reference

1. Chen, Y., Sion, R.: To cloud or not to cloud?: musings on costs and viability. In: Proceedings of the 2nd ACM Symposium on Cloud Computing, SOCC '11, pp. 29:1–29:7. ACM, New York (2011)

Vision Papers

Data Security – Challenges and Research Opportunities

Elisa Bertino[✉]

Cyber Center, CS Department, and CERIAS, Purdue University,
West Lafayette, IN, USA
bertino@cs.purdue.edu

Abstract. The proliferation of web-based applications and information systems, and recent trends such as cloud computing and outsourced data management, have increased the exposure of data and made security more difficult. In this paper we briefly discuss open issues, such as data protection from insider threat and how to reconcile security and privacy, and outline research directions.

1 Introduction

Issues around data confidentiality and privacy are under greater focus than ever before as ubiquitous internet access exposes critical corporate data and personal information to new security threats. On one hand, data sharing across different parties and for different purposes is crucial for many applications, including homeland security, medical research, and environmental protection. The availability of "big data" technologies makes it possible to quickly analyze huge data sets and is thus further pushing the massive collection of data. On the other hand, the combination of multiple datasets may allow parties holding these datasets to infer sensitive information. Pervasive data gathering from multiple data sources and devices, such as smart phones and smart power meters, further exacerbates this tension.

Techniques for fine-grained and context-based access control are crucial for achieving data confidentiality and privacy. Depending on the specific use of data, e.g. operational purposes or analytical purposes, data anonymization techniques may also be applied. An important challenge in this context is represented by the *insider threat*, that is, data misuses by individuals who have access to data for carrying on their organizational functions, and thus possess the necessary authorizations to access proprietary or sensitive data. Protection against insider requires not only fine-grained and context-based access control but also anomaly detection systems, able to detect unusual patterns of data access, and data user surveillance systems, able to monitor user actions and habits in cyber space – for example whether a data user is active on social networks. Notice that the adoption of anomaly detection and surveillance systems entails data user privacy issues and therefore a challenge is how to reconcile data protection with data user privacy. It is important to point out that when dealing with data privacy, one has to distinguish between *data subjects*, that is, the users to whom the data is related, and *data users*, that is, the users accessing the data. Privacy

W. Jonker and M. Petković (Eds.): SDM 2013, LNCS 8425, pp. 9–13, 2014.
DOI: 10.1007/978-3-319-06811-4_2, © Springer International Publishing Switzerland 2014

of both categories of user is important, even though only few approaches have been proposed for data user privacy [6, 8, 9].

Data security is not, however, limited to data confidentiality and privacy. As data is often used for critical decision making, data trustworthiness is a crucial requirement. Data needs to be protected from unauthorized modifications. Its provenance must be available and certified. Data must be accurate, complete and up-do-date. Comprehensive data trustworthiness solutions are difficult to achieve as they need to combine different techniques, such as digital signatures, semantic integrity, data quality techniques, as well taking into account data semantics. Notice also that assuring data trustworthiness may require a tight control on data management processes which has privacy implications.

In what follows we briefly elaborate on the above issues and research challenges.

2 Access Control and Protection from Insider Threat

From a conceptual point of view, an access control mechanism typically includes a reference monitor that checks that requested accesses by *subjects* to protected *objects* to perform certain actions on these objects are allowed according to the access control policies. The decision taken by the access control mechanism is referred to as *access control decision*. Of course, in order to be effective access control mechanisms must support fine-grained access control that refers to finely tuning the permitted accesses along different dimensions, including data object contents, time and location of the access, purpose of the access. By properly restricting the contexts of the possible accesses one can reduce improper data accesses and the opportunities for insiders to steal data. To address such a requirement, extended access control models have been proposed, including time-based access control models, location-based access control models, purpose-based access control models, and attribute-based access control models that restrict data accesses with respect to time periods, locations, purpose of data usage, and user identity attributes [8], respectively.

Even though the area of access control has been widely investigated [2], there are many open research directions, including how to reconcile access control with privacy, and how to design access control models and mechanisms for social networks and mobile devices. Many advanced access control models require that information, such as the location of the user requiring access or user identity attributes [3], be provided to the access control monitor. The acquisition of such information may result in privacy breaches and the use of cloud for managing the data and enforcing access control policies on the data further increases the risks for data users of being target of spear phishing attacks. The challenge is how to perform access control while at the same time maintaining the privacy of the user personal and context information [6, 8].

Social networks and mobile devices acquire a large variety of information about individuals; therefore access control mechanisms are needed to control with which parties this information is shared. Also today user owned mobile devices are increasingly being used for job-related tasks and thus store enterprise confidential data. The main issue is that, unlike conventional enterprise environments in which administrators and other specialized staff are in charge of deploying access control policies, in social networks and mobile devices end-users are in charge of deploying their own personal access control policies. The main challenge is how to make sure that devices storing enterprise confidential data enforce the enterprise access control policies and to make sure that un-trusted applications are unable to access this data.

It is important to point out that access control alone may not be sufficient to protect data against insider threat as an insider may have a legitimate permission for certain data accesses. It is therefore crucial to be able determine whether an access, even though is granted by the access control mechanism, is "anomalous" with respect to data accesses typical of the job function of the data user and/or the usual data access patterns. For example, consider a user that has the permission to read an entire table in a database and assume that for his/her job function, the user only needs to access a few entries a day and does so during working hours. With respect to such access pattern, an access performed after office hours and resulting in the download of the entire table would certainly be anomalous and needs to be flagged. Initial solutions to anomaly detection for data accesses have been proposed [5]. However these may not be effective against sophisticated attacks and needs to be complemented by techniques such as separation-of-duties [1] and data flow control.

3 Data Trustworthiness

The problem of providing "trustworthy" data to users is an inherently difficult problem which often depends on the application and data semantics as well as on the current context and situation. In many cases, it is crucial to provide users and applications not only with the needed data, but with also an evaluation indicating how much the data can be trusted. Being able to do so is particularly challenging especially when large amounts of data are generated and continuously transmitted. Solutions for improving data, like those found in data quality, may be very expensive and require access to data sources which may have access restrictions, because of data sensitivity. Also even when one adopts methodologies to assure that the data is of good quality, attackers may still be able to inject incorrect data; therefore, it is important to assess the damage resulting from the use of such data, to track and contain the spread of errors, and to recover. The many challenges for assuring data trustworthiness require articulated solutions combining different approaches and techniques including data integrity, data quality, record linkage [4], and data provenance [10]. Initial approaches for sensor networks [7] have been proposed that apply game theory techniques with the goal of determine which sensor nodes need to be "hardened" so to assure that data has a certain level of trustworthiness. However many issues need to be addressed, such as protection again colluding attackers, articulated metrics for "data trustworthiness", privacy-preserving data matching and correlation techniques.

4 Reconciling Data Security and Privacy

As already mentioned, assuring data security requires among other measures creating user activity profiles for anomaly detection, collecting data provenance, and context information such as user location. Much of this information is privacy sensitive and security breaches or data misuses by administrators may lead to privacy breaches. Also users may not feel comfortable with their personal data, habits and behavior being collected for security purposes. It would thus seem that security and privacy are conflicting requirements. However this is not necessarily true. Notable examples of approaches reconciling data security and privacy include:

- Privacy-preserving attribute-based fine-grained access control for data on a cloud [8]. These techniques allow one to enforce access control policies taking into account identity information about users for data stored in a public cloud without requiring this information to be disclosed to the cloud, thus preserving user privacy.
- Privacy-preserving location-based role-based access control [6]. These techniques allow one to enforce access control based on location, so that users can access certain data only when located in secure locations associated with the protected data. Such techniques do not require however that the user locations be disclosed to the access control systems, thus preserving user location privacy.

Those are just some examples referring to access control. Of course one needs to devise privacy-preserving protocols for other security functions. Recent advances in encryption techniques, such as homomorphic encryption, may allow one to compute functions on encrypted data and thus may be used as a building block for constructing such protocols.

Acknowledgments. The research reported in this paper has been partially supported by NSF under awards CNS-1111512, CNS-1016722, CNS-0964294.

References

1. Bertino, E.: Data Protection from Insider Threats: Synthesis Lectures on Data Management. Morgan & Claypool Publishers, San Rafael (2012)
2. Bertino, E., Ghinita, G., Kamra, A.: Access control for databases: concepts and systems. Found. Trends Databases **3**(1–2), 1–148 (2011)
3. Bertino, E., Takahashi, K.: Identity Management: Concepts, Technologies, and Systems. Artech House, Boston (2010)
4. Inan, A., Kantarcioglu, M., Ghinita, G., Bertino, E.: A hybrid approach to record matching. IEEE Trans. Dependable Sec. Comp. **9**(5), 684–698 (2012)
5. Kamra, A., Bertino, E.: Design and implementation of an intrusion response system for relational databases. IEEE Trans. Knowl. Data Eng. **23**(6), 875–888 (2011)
6. Kirkpatrick, M.S., Ghinita, G., Bertino, E.: Privacy-preserving enforcement of spatially aware RBAC. IEEE Trans. Dependable Sec. Comp. **9**(5), 627–640 (2012)
7. Lim, H.S., Ghinita, G., Bertino, E., Kantarciolgu, M.: A game-theoretic approach for high assurance data. In: Proceedings of the IEEE 28th International Conference on Data Engineering, Washington, DC, USA, 1–5 April 2012
8. Nabeel, M., Shang, N., Bertino, E.: Privacy preserving policy based content sharing in public clouds. IEEE Trans. Knowl. Data Eng. (to appear)

9. Nabeel, M., Shang, N., Bertino, E.: Efficient privacy preserving content based publish subscribe systems. In: Proceedings of the 17th ACM Symposium on Access Control Models and Technologies (SACMAT), Newark, NJ, 20–22 June 2012
10. Sultana, S., Shehab, M., Bertino, E.: Secure provenance transmission for streaming data. IEEE Trans. Knowl. Data Eng. **25**(8), 1890–1903 (2013)

Research Challenges to Secure the Future Internet

Jan Camenisch[✉]

IBM Research – Zurich, Säumerstrasse 4, 8803 Rüschlikon, Switzerland
jca@zurich.ibm.com

Abstract. This article puts forth a number of research challenges that need to be overcome to secure the future digital world and protect the people living in it.

1 A New World is Shaping

The Internet has transformed our environment and how we interact with each other dramatically. Soon all things surrounding us will be part of the Internet, producing, processing, proving, and consuming enormous amounts of data. However, all these devices, their operating systems, and applications (often distributed over several devices and administrative boundaries) are very complex, and even experts understand only parts of these systems. Thus, managing and securing them is a huge challenge, in particular for private users and small enterprises who are not and cannot afford to hire IT security professionals. Making our future infrastructure secure and trustworthy will require novel approaches and new technologies. We discuss some of the research challenges involved.

Authorisation, Authentication, and Encryption and Data Governance. The future infrastructure will consist of many distributed systems composed of many different kinds of devices controlled by many different parties. It seems impossible to protect all devices and system, virtually or even physically. Therefore secure authorisation and communication, and protecting data at rest are of vital importance. It is necessary to authenticate and encrypt every single bit as well as explicitly define who is allowed to do what with the bit, i.e., to attach a data usage policy to each bit. However, authenticating every bit might result in decreasing the amount of privacy and hence in a potential decrease of security.

To alleviate this, privacy protecting authentication mechanisms such as anonymous credentials should be applied. Although such authentication and encryption mechanisms do exist and data usage control is an active area of research, much more research is needed until these technologies can be used to secure large distributed systems. Research topics here include how to make such complex technologies usable and how to deploy them, what infrastructure is needed to help users protect and maintain their private data, and how users can keep control of their data and understands for what and how their data are used.

W. Jonker and M. Petković (Eds.): SDM 2013, LNCS 8425, pp. 14–17, 2014.
DOI: 10.1007/978-3-319-06811-4_3, © Springer International Publishing Switzerland 2014 2014

Distributing Services. While the Internet is a distributed system, most of the applications running on it are centralized with browsers as standardized clients. The obvious advantages of a centralized system with standardized clients include easier application maintenance as well as easier management and processing of application data. From a security and privacy point of view, however, a centralized system not desirable as it is a unique point of failure and, by having all data at a central location, it is an attractive target for attackers - be it insiders or outsiders. Thus, an important research direction here is how decentralised applications that protect privacy but are as easy to run and maintain as centralised systems can be designed. Research topics here include what kind of protocols and APIs need to be specified and standardized to this end (similar to the IP protocol for the transport layer) and how different services offered by different parties can be combined in an easy and secure way.

2   Information Security Research Challenges

It seems that the basic security technologies such as encryption and digital signature schemes are well understood today, and no further research is needed. However, a closer analysis shows that traditional encryption and signature schemes very often fulfil the application requirements only partially, and thus different or modified cryptographic primitives are required. Moreover, means to efficiently compose different secured components into larger systems while maintaining security are not yet very well understood. Let us expand on this.

New Cryptographic Primitives. One research direction is to analyze different application scenarios carefully, deriving the security requirements, and then designing appropriate cryptographic primitives that meet them. Also, using cryptographic primitives to secure applications means that cryptographic keys need to be managed. This is already very demanding for IT professionals and even more so for ordinary users. It seems that enabling users to manage their keys (and other sensitive data) requires fundamentally new cryptographic primitives, protocols, and policy languages. Mechanisms are required that allow humans to securely store and retrieve cryptographic keys based on a single human-memorizable password, based on biometrics, or based on hardware tokens. In addition mechanisms are needed that enable end users to manage their various cryptographic keys and their encrypted data via these keys.

Security Modelling and Composition. Properly defining the security requirements of a cryptographic function, protocol, or full system is far from straightforward. Also, proving that these requirements are meet by a realization is very error-prone. To master these complexities, several security composition models have been proposed. However, these models are still being developed and so far mostly concentrate on cryptographic protocols rather than on more general, security-relevant systems. Thus, research needs to come up with more mature models, that are easy to use and, ideally, such that proofs in these models can be automatically checked, hopefully even in realtime when systems being configured and modified.

3   Getting Security and Privacy-Protecting Technologies Used

Many security and privacy-protecting technologies are quite complex and have a plethora of different features that often are counterintuitive. This makes them challenging to deploy and to use. To address this, the complexity of these technologies need to be reduced and their possibilities communicated to the various stakeholders.

Usable Cryptographic Libraries. Despite the large number of different cryptographic primitives and schemes that the research literature provides, only very few of them are used in the real world. One reason for this might be the lack of software libraries that provide cryptographic primitives other than plain encryption, signature, and key exchange. Therefore, research is needed to determine what kind of cryptographic primitives are most useful for building higher-level protocols, to develop a suitable abstraction to render them easier to understand and use, and to design APIs that are as simple as possible and less error-prone in their use.

Professional Stakeholders. Proper security and privacy have to become core requirements for any mechanism or application that is built. When designing an application, the requirements put forth are often a reflection of what the person(s) in charge understands of the available technologies and how they can be employed. This includes the way business processes are designed and how they are implemented technically. It is therefore essentials that the people in the entire design chain be aware of the possibilities of state-of-the-art security technologies, in particular the privacy protecting and enabling ones. The same is true for policy makers: to be able to draft new regulations and laws that govern our digital world, they need to be aware of the possibilities of the available technologies, their dangers and their merits, and how they can be used or abused.

To this end, research is needed to analyze different application scenarios and to find alternative realizations that are more secure and protect the privacy of the users better. This will most likely require the development of new technologies or at least the innovative use of existing ones. This will demonstrate the feasibility of such approaches on the one hand and drive research and innovation on the other hand.

Human Computers Interfaces and Education of End Users. To foster market adoption of security and privacy-protecting technologies, the end users need to be made aware of the risks of the current technologies and how these risks could be addressed with alternative technologies and mechanisms. So, research needs to develop mental models that are understandable and enable HCI designs (which again requires a lot of research) so that users can effectively control and apply the technologies (e.g., to manage and safely use their data and keys).

Economic Models and Security & Privacy. A large part of the services offered on the Internet are free of charge and financed by making use of personal information that the users reveal, voluntarily or not, when using the Internet. Thus, service providers are motivated to learn more information about their users so that they can target their advertizements better and hence invest in better methods to acquire such data. To increase security, alternative economic models and menthols need to be developed that do not require the user to reveal personal data or only very little.

4   Conclusion

The speed with which the Internet evolves and new applications get introduced and embraced makes it very challenging to address the emerging security and privacy problems, in particular because privacy and security are too often not taken into consideration by design. Despite this, security and privacy research is still very relevant and, indeed, the general public is becoming increasingly aware of the need of proper security and privacy protection. Thus one can expect the security and privacy research community to grow in the future, and there is certainly no lack of interesting and challenging problems to be addressed, some of which we have pointed out in this brief article.

Security and Privacy of Data in a Cloud

Sushil Jajodia$^{(\boxtimes)}$

Center for Secure Information Systems,
George Mason University, Fairfax, VA, USA
jajodia@gmu.edu

Abstract. The goals of this brief note are to describe some of the research progress that has been made to date and elaborate on the fundamental challenges facing the research community in security and privacy of data stored in a cloud.

Keywords: Cloud security · Data security · Data privacy

1 Introduction

The major driver for move to public clouds is the numerous advantages from a data owner perspective over the traditional model of doing computing on an owned infrastructure. These advantages include elimination of physical infrastructure management, reduced operational costs, and flexibility in matching computational resources to the demands. However, the cloud computing paradigm introduces a host of new issues with respect to security and privacy that are not yet well understood.

Inspired by the pioneering paper by Hacigümüş et al. [16], much of the work carried out in the context of *database as a service* paradigm is applicable to the cloud. Under this paradigm, a data owner delegates the management and storage of a data collection, possibly including sensitive information that can be selectively accessed by authorized users, to an honest-but-curious external server (An honest-but-curious server is trusted to properly manage the data and make them available when needed but it is not trusted to read the data content).

The remainder of this note provides an overview of the main data security and privacy issues that characterize the aforementioned scenario along with possible solutions. It also briefly mentions some open issues that need further investigation.

2 Data Confidentiality

The first approach proposed to provide confidentiality of outsourced data is to wrap a protective layer of encryption around sensitive data to counteract both outside attacks and the curiosity of the server itself (e.g., [4,16,18,26]).

W. Jonker and M. Petković (Eds.): SDM 2013, LNCS 8425, pp. 18–22, 2014.
DOI: 10.1007/978-3-319-06811-4_4, © Springer International Publishing Switzerland 2014

To minimize the use of encryption and make access to outsourced data more efficient, recent proposals combine fragmentation and encryption techniques [1,6–8]. These approaches are based on the observation that often data are not sensitive per se but what is sensitive is their association with other data. It is therefore sufficient to protect sensitive associations to preserve data confidentiality.

Several open issues still remain to be addressed. For instance, the fragmentation process should take into account dependencies among attributes in the original relation since they could be exploited by adversaries to reconstruct the association among attributes appearing in different fragments. As an example, the specialty of a patient's doctor (an oncologist) may reveal the disease the patient suffers from (cancer). Another open problem is that in real world scenarios, data collections are subject to frequent changes whereas the current research has focused on the confidentiality of static datasets.

3   Efficient Query Evaluation

In the last few years, several techniques have been proposed to support the server-side evaluation of a wide set of selection conditions and SQL clauses when the outsourced relation is completely encrypted. These solutions complement the encrypted relation with additional metadata, called indexes, on which queries are evaluated at the server side [2,9,15–17,27]. The main challenge that must be addressed in the definition of indexing techniques is balancing efficiency and confidentiality: more precise indexes result in more efficient query execution, but at the price of a greater exposure to possible confidentiality violations.

Besides the alternative indexing techniques for encrypted data and for efficiently evaluating queries on fragmented data, one open issue that remains is the possibility of combining fragmentation and indexing approaches [10]. In fact, fragmentation does not permit delegation of the evaluation of conditions involving attributes that do not appear in plaintext in a fragment. The association of indexes to fragments could nicely fill this gap, but should be carefully designed to prevent information leakage caused by the plaintext representation in a fragment of an attribute indexed in another.

4   Access Control Enforcement

The solutions proposed to enforce access control restrictions on outsourced data without the data owners intervention are based on integrating access control and encryption [11,12].

Most of the problems studied for the enforcement of read privileges need to be extended to both read and write privileges. It is also necessary to devise efficient approaches for managing policy updates without any involvement of the data owner, and techniques for protecting the confidentiality of the policy when read and write operations are restricted to arbitrary subsets of users.

5   Data Integrity

Data integrity can be provided at different granularity levels: table, attribute, tuple, or cell level. The integrity verification at the table and attribute level is expensive since it can be performed by the client only downloading the whole table/column. Data integrity at the cell level suffers from a high verification overhead. For these reasons, the majority of the current proposals provide data integrity at the tuple level.

Current approaches for providing integrity guarantees to externally stored data typically adopt signature techniques [5, 21]. These solutions are, however, computationally expensive both for the data owner and for clients. It would be useful to have alternative approaches based on less expensive techniques that permit authorized users to efficiently check data integrity.

6   Completeness, Freshness, and Correctness of Query Results

Although the problem of providing guarantees of completeness and freshness of query results is of increasing interest [13, 19, 20, 22–24, 28, 29, 32], there are still many aspects that need to be further investigated. Current solutions consider simple select-from-where SQL queries operating on a single relation only; it is necessary to assess the correctness and completeness of the result of more complex queries (e.g., queries including group by and having clauses). Probabilistic approaches [28–30] provide a good trade-off between completeness guarantee and efficiency in query evaluation. It would be interesting to develop efficient approaches that provide absolute certainty of completeness and freshness of query results, while limiting the computational overhead.

7   Cheap and Lazy Cloud Providers and Side Channels

There are two other threats that deserve mentioning. First, in a cloud, service level agreements (SLAs) serve as the foundation for the expected level of service between the data owner and the cloud. However, a *cheap and lazy* cloud provider [3] may fail to enforce an SLA due to either cost cutting or negligence. To detect this, it is important to devise methods to allow data owners to verify if the cloud is abiding by an SLA. Second, it is possible for a malicious virtual machine (VM) to establish a side-channel if two VMs can share the same physical resource [25]. This means that isolation in a cloud must be enforced carefully to prevent information leakage.

There is limited progress towards addressing these problems. Bowers et al. [3] provide a way for a data owner to verify that the cloud stores a file in a fault-tolerant manner by storing a fixed numbers of replicas specified in the SLA. Wang et al. [31] present a mechanism for data owners to verify that the disk storage isolation is being enforced by the cloud.

Acknowledgement. My collaborators – Pierangela Samarati, Sabrina De Capitani di Vimercati, Sara Foresti, Stefano Paraboschi, and Zhan Wang – deserve much of the credit for the technical contributions summarized in this paper. See [14,31] for greater details on many of the ideas in this note.

This research was funded in part by the US Army Research Office under MURI grant W911NF-09-1-0525 and DURIP grant W911NF-11-1-0340. Part of the work was performed while Sushil Jajodia was a Visiting Researcher at the US Army Research Laboratory.

References

1. Aggarwal, G., Bawa, M., Ganesan, P., Garcia-Molina, H., Kenthapadi, K., Motwani, R., Srivastava, U., Thomas, D., Xu, Y.: Two can keep a secret: a distributed architecture for secure database services. In: Proceedings of CIDR, Asilomar, CA (2005)
2. Agrawal, R., Kierman, J., Srikant, R., Xu, Y.: Order preserving encryption for numeric data. In: Proceedings of SIGMOD, Paris, France (2004)
3. Bowers, K.D., van Dijk, M., Juels, A., Oprea, A., Rivest, R.L.: How to tell if your cloud files are vulnerable to drive crashes. In: Proceedings of ACM CCS (2011)
4. Ceselli, A., Damiani, E., De Capitani di Vimercati, S., Samarati, P.: Modeling and assessing inference exposure in encrypted databases. ACM TISSEC **8**(1), 119–152 (2005)
5. Boneh, D., Gentry, C., Lynn, B., Shacham, H.: Aggregate and verifiably encrypted signatures from bilinear maps. In: Proceedings of EUROCRYPT 2003, Warsaw, Poland (2003)
6. Ciriani, V., De Capitani, S., Samarati, P.: Enforcing confidentiality constraints on sensitive databases with lightweight trusted clients. In: Proceedings of DBSec, Montreal, Canada (2009)
7. Ciriani, V., De Capitani di Vimercati, S., Foresti, S., Jajodia, S., Paraboschi, S., Samarati, P.: Keep a few: outsourcing data while maintaining confidentiality. In: Backes, M., Ning, P. (eds.) ESORICS 2009. LNCS, vol. 5789, pp. 440–455. Springer, Heidelberg (2009)
8. Ciriani, V., De Capitani di Vimercati, S., Foresti, S., Jajodia, S., Paraboschi, S., Samarati, P.: Combining fragmentation and encryption to protect privacy in data storage. ACM TISSEC **13**(3), 22:1–22:33 (2010)
9. Damiani, E., De Capitani, S., Samarati, P.: Balancing confidentiality and efficiency in untrusted relational DBMSs. In: Proceedings of CCS, Washington, DC (2003)
10. De Capitani, S., di Vimercati, S., Foresti, S., Jajodia, S.: On information leakage by indexes over data fragments. In: Proceedings of PrivDB, Brisbane, Australia (2013)
11. De Capitani di Vimercati, S., Foresti, S., Jajodia, S., Paraboschi, S., Samarati, P.: Encryption policies for regulating access to outsourced data. ACM TODS **35**(2), 12:1–12:46 (2010)
12. De Capitani di Vimercati, S., Foresti, S., Jajodia, S., Paraboschi, S., Samarati, P.: Support for Write privileges on outsourced data. In: Gritzalis, D., Furnell, S., Theoharidou, M. (eds.) SEC 2012. IFIP AICT, vol. 376, pp. 199–210. Springer, Heidelberg (2012)
13. Devanbu, P.T., Gertz, M., Martel, C.U., Stubblebine, S.G.. Authentic third-party data publication. In: Proceedings of DBSec 2000 (2000)

14. De Capitani di Vimercati, S., Foresti, S., Jajodia, S., Samarati, P.: Database security and privacy. In: Topi, H. (ed.) Computing Handbook, Third Edition: Information Systems and Information Technology, vol. 2. Taylor & Francis, Boca Raton (2013)

15. Ganapathy, V., Thomas, D., Feder, T., Garcia-Molina, H., Motwani, R.: Distributing data for secure database services. In: Proceedings of PAIS, Uppsala, Sweden (2011)

16. Hacigümüş, H., Iyer, B., Mehrotra, S.: Providing database as a service. In: Proceedings of ICDE, San Jose, CA (2002)

17. Hacıgümüş, H., Iyer, B., Mehrotra, S.: Efficient execution of aggregation queries over encrypted relational databases. In: Lee, Y.J., Li, J., Whang, K.-Y., Lee, D. (eds.) DASFAA 2004. LNCS, vol. 2973, pp. 125–136. Springer, Heidelberg (2004)

18. Hacigümüş, H., Iyer, B., Mehrotra, S., Li, C.: Executing SQL over encrypted data in the database-service-provider model. In: Proceedings of SIGMOD, Madison, WI (2002)

19. Li, F., Hadjieleftheriou, M., Kollios, G., Reyzin, L.: Dynamic authenticated index structures for outsourced databases. In: Proceedings of SIGMOD, Chicago, IL (2006)

20. Liu, R., Wang, H.: Integrity verification of outsourced XML databases. In: Proceedings of CSE, Vancouver, Canada (2009)

21. Mykletun, E., Narasimha, M., Tsudik, G.: Authentication and integrity in outsourced databases. ACM TOS 2(2), 107–138 (2006)

22. Narasimha, M., Tsudik, G.: DSAC: integrity for outsourced databases with signature aggregation and chaining. In: Proceedings of CIKM, Bremen, Germany, 31 Oct–5 Nov 2005 (2005)

23. Pang, H., Jain, A., Ramamritham, K., Tan, K.L.: Verifying completeness of relational query results in data publishing. In: Proceedings of SIGMOD, Baltimore, MA (2005)

24. Pang, H., Tan, K.L.: Authenticating query results in edge computing. In: Proceedings of ICDE, Boston, MA (2004)

25. Ristenpart, T., Tromer, E., Shacham, H., Savage, S.: Hey, you, get off of my cloud: exploring information leakage in third-party compute clouds. In: Proceedings of ACM CCS (2009)

26. Samarati, P., De Capitani, S.: Data protection in outsourcing scenarios: issues and directions. In: Proceedings of ASIACCS, China (2010)

27. Wang, H., Lakshmanan, L.V.S.: Efficient secure query evaluation over encrypted XML databases. In: Proceedings of VLDB, Seoul, Korea (2006)

28. Wang, H., Yin, J., Perng, C., Yu, P.S.: Dual encryption for query integrity assurance. In: Proceedings of CIKM, Napa Valley, CA (2008)

29. Xie, M., Wang, H., Yin, J., Meng, X.: Integrity auditing of outsourced data. In: Proceedings of VLDB, Vienna, Austria (2007)

30. Xie, M., Wang, H., Yin, J., Meng, X.: Providing freshness guarantees for outsourced databases. In: Proceedings of EDBT, Nantes, France (2008)

31. Wang, Z., Sun, K., Jajodia, S., Jing, J.: Disk storage isolation and verification in cloud. In: Proceedings of IEEE Globecom, Anaheim, CA (2012)

32. Yang, Y., Papadias, D., Papadopoulos, S., Kalnis, P.: Authenticated join processing in outsourced databases. In: Proceedings of SIGMOD, Providence, RI, 29 June–2 July 2009 (2009)

The Future of Information Security Research: Cryptology and Beyond

Bart Preneel[✉]

Department of Electrical Engineering-ESAT/COSIC,
KU Leuven and iMinds,
Kasteelpark Arenberg 10 Bus 2452, 3001 Leuven, Belgium
bart.preneel@esat.kuleuven.be

Abstract. This paper reflects on the state of the art in cryptology and information security. It considers the main achievements and shortcomings of research and identifies the major challenges for the future. It explores which research approaches have a high potential to evolve from academic ideas to practical solutions. The paper concludes by discussing how the deployment of more secure and reliable IT systems requires a complete re-engineering including new architectures; it also sketches the broader societal context of such a redesign.

As scientific discipline, cryptology was born during World War II with the seminal work of Shannon. In the 1970s, the academic research in the area took off, with the invention of public-key cryptology by Diffie and Hellman. During the last four decades, cryptology has developed into a mature scientific discipline with sub-disciplines focusing on foundations, cryptographic algorithms and protocols, and secure and efficient implementations. The dramatic reduction in cost of hardware and communication and the development of the Internet have resulted in the processing and storage of huge amounts of personal data; this has motivated the mass deployment of cryptology during the past two decades.

In spite of these successes there are major challenges ahead. While cryptographic theory has developed solid foundations, most of this theory deals with reduction proofs, that show that a cryptographic primitive is secure if a certain problem is hard. It has been noted that some of these proofs have shortcomings in the sense that the model used is not realistic, or that the reduction is not tight. However, it seems that the main issue is that as a community, we don't know which problems are hard; even for problems we believe to be hard it is very difficult to make reliable estimates for the difficulty of concrete instances.

Symmetric cryptographic algorithms seem to be rather mature: the block cipher AES and the hash function SHA-2 are widely deployed and one can expect that SHA-3 (Keccak) will find its way into products quickly. For stream ciphers, the field is more diverse but the eSTREAM competition has resulted in several promising designs. The short term challenges are how to phase out many older and weaker algorithms (such as A5/1, E0, Keeloq, MD2, and MD5), the design of more efficient and versatile schemes for authenticated encryption, and the further reduction of cost of these algorithms (a.k.a. lightweight cryptography).

W. Jonker and M. Petković (Eds.): SDM 2013, LNCS 8425, pp. 23–27, 2014.
DOI: 10.1007/978-3-319-06811-4_5, © Springer International Publishing Switzerland 2014

The long term question is whether we can find novel techniques to cryptanalyze the current schemes or whether we can start building evidence (or even proofs) that these constructions offer long term security.

One particular threat to the currently widely deployed systems is the development of quantum computers. Twenty years ago, these we considered to be exotic objects; today it is clear that substantial progress has been made. It remains an open question whether or not quantum computers will be able to break realistic key lengths for public-key algorithms in the next twenty years. However, if they can, public-key algorithms – and thus our information security infrastructure – will be in deep trouble. Moreover, it should be realized that changing a global infrastructure can take 10–20 years (or even more); and some data such as medical, financial, or government data requires confidentiality for 50 years or more. In view of this, more resources need to be spent on the development of concrete proposals for public-key algorithms that resist quantum computers. There has been some excellent research in the past decade in this area, so this topic is no longer "new" or "hot." On the other hand, interest for this issue in the industry is low, as the time horizon of this research lies beyond 2020.

In addition to the risks created by novel computers, the open cryptographic community learned in the past decades that, even if cryptographic systems are mathematically secure, their implementations can be vulnerable. One potentially weak element are the Application Programming Interfaces (APIs) to software libraries and hardware modules. Attackers can also exploit physical phenomena, such as side channels (timing, power, electromagnetic radiation) or active attacks such as the deliberate injection of faults in the hardware (e.g. by voltage glitches or laser pulses). There has been a large body of research on securing implementations by masking or hiding information and by verifying calculations to detect injected faults; there also have been initial ideas on how to create implementations with a security proof (under the name leakage-resilient implementations). However, the models considered in theory are far from practice and even the best *ad hoc* solutions are too inefficient. This means that cryptographic implementations have to switch to "security by obscurity": while the algorithm used is known, the details on how it is implemented have to remain secret – revealing the (limited) countermeasures against implementation attacks that are present would allow to break the system. There is no doubt that further research is needed to create better models and more secure implementations.

It took about 20 years for the breakthrough research on public-key cryptology of the late 1970s to become widely deployed. This required a major engineering effort. Since then, at cryptology conferences an ever growing number of more complex protocols is being presented. The challenge is to understand how one can build up a large body of schemes and study how their security relates. But few of those schemes make it to implementations – either because there is no need for them or because the application developers do not understand the benefits. The broader research agenda however that is being pursued is highly relevant: while historically cryptography was developed to secure communication channels and later on to protect local storage, cryptography is much more powerful. With advanced cryptographic tools, one can replace a central trusted party by a distributed system. The use of centralized trusted parties seem to have been essential for modern societies and the advent of information technologies has only exacerbated this trend: in application such as auctions, search, recommendation systems, road pricing, e-commerce, and in many security systems centralized parties play a key role. However, a properly designed cryptographic protocol allows to create a completely different design, that is fully distributed and in which no central party needs to be fully trusted. The system optimally protects the interests of each party and works if the majority of the players is honest. As there is no central party, this kind of design can be much more robust against attacks either by hackers or by governments. While the first designs brought enormous overhead in terms of communication and storage, there has been tremendous progress and some proofs of concepts and even real deployments have materialized. One can compare this approach to peer-to-peer distribution versus centralized distribution, with as difference that much stronger security guarantees are provided and a broader range of applications can be covered. It is clear that implementing such systems will be extremely hard: the technological challenges are daunting and one will always pay a performance penalty compared to fully centralized systems. One can also question whether cryptographers can ever convince society that such an approach is indeed better. Moreover, the large incumbents and several governments have nothing to gain by such an approach that undermines their power.

While cryptology is essential for information security and privacy, it is only a very small part of the very complex security puzzle. There has been a substantial amount of excellent work on information security, but the discipline itself seems to lack maturity. This may be because information security is much broader than cryptology; moreover, it is more closely coupled to the ever changing information infrastructure that is deployed with minimal or no security. In this environment new programming languages, frameworks, and system architectures are deployed continuously. As an example, browsers have evolved from simple viewing programs to sophisticated software that is more complex than an operating system from the 1980s. On the one hand, innovative security ideas are being incorporated, but each new development opens up a plethora of new weaknesses. The situation can be summed up with a quote from A. Shamir: "In information security, we are winning some battles but losing the war."

While security and privacy by design are a common mantra, very few systems have been designed with security or privacy as dominating factors: it is well understood that deployed systems are driven by economic factors, and in most cases it is preferred to have a successful but not so secure system that can be patched later, over a much more secure system that arrives one year too late in the market. Once a system or infrastructure is successful, updating its security is extremely difficult – this has been compared to changing the wheels on a bicycle while one is driving it. The overall solution is to patch the most blatant holes, have centralized detection and monitoring to go after abusive attacks and keep fingers crossed that no disastrous attack will happen. This approach has worked rather well for the first two decades of the Internet as a mass medium, but we are now witnessing its limitations. In particular, as more and more of our critical infrastructure goes online (very often with very limited or even no protection) and the Internet and cyber world are developing as the theater not only for crime but also for terrorism attacks and war, one can question whether the past approach that seemed adequate for e-commerce and business infrastructure is sufficient to build an information society on.

If the answer is no, the discipline of information security and privacy engineering should be further developed to create solid long term solutions. This is only possible if we start re-thinking the way we architect, develop, and evolve systems: security and privacy considerations should be one of the key drivers of an infrastructure that is too big to fail. It is important to keep in mind that "architecture is politics": the choice of an architecture is not a purely technical decision, but it is determined by and determines power relations in the information society. The best way to avoid huge privacy breaches is by stopping to collect massive amounts of personal data. For reliability and correctness, we can learn from the aviation and space industry, that have developed advanced methods to create reliable and complex systems (in spite of this, it seems that they use insecure communication channels). Of course we would need a more cost effective approach that can deliver similar results.

It is not within the scope of this position paper to give more concrete answers, but some of the elements that are needed are obvious: the only systems we can make secure are simple systems; hence we need a better understanding of how to reduce complexity and how to put together secure systems from well understood and simple building blocks. This approach has been used in the past, but probably deserves more attention. Another element that needs more attention is modularity: so far we have failed to deliver on this, as upgrading a cryptographic algorithm or protocol is much more complex than it should be. Finally, we should question the current approach of extreme centralization, where all the data and control of a system are brought to a single place: we have learned that eventually these systems will be compromised with dramatic consequences for both privacy and security.

The above problems are well understood by the security community, but somehow we have failed to make progress. On the one hand, research tends to focus on the "find a hole and patch it" game, that brings short term success. On the other hand, there are very few drivers to start from scratch and develop systems that are more robust, secure, and reliable. Moreover, this would require a large scale international collaboration effort between industry and academia, which is complex to manage.

It would be very interesting to study how society can be transformed to deal in a more effective way with large scale risks and vulnerabilities that are created by the information infrastructure.[1] This is a complex problem with economical, psychological, sociological, political and legal dimensions. While there is an

---

[1] The same applies of course to our financial infrastructure and to the problems of energy supply and global warming.

understanding that liability could play a role as the key driver to align the market players, it seems very difficult to conceive how one could assign liability in a complex system in which billions of subsystems interact. Moreover, for privacy the problem is even more challenging, as some of the damage by revealing sensitive personal data can create irreversible harm. Overall this would require a thorough redesign of the complete architecture of our ICT systems to make them more robust and distributed; distributed cryptography could play an important role here. But it seems likely that society will only be prepared to pay the price for this after a major disaster.

Acknowledgements. This work was supported in part by the Research Council KU Leuven (GOA TENSE/11/007), by the Flemish Government (FWO WET G.0213.11N and IWT MobCOM), and by the European Commission through the ICT programme under contract FP7-ICT-2013-10-SEP-210076296 PRACTICE.

Where Security Research Should Go in the Next Decade

Kai Rannenberg[✉]

Deutsche Telekom Chair of Mobile Business & Multilateral Security,
Goethe University Frankfurt, Frankfurt, Germany
Kai.Rannenberg@m-chair.de
http://www.m-chair.de

Abstract. In 2004 the series of annual Secure Data Management workshops as part of VLDB began, so SDM can now celebrate its 10th edition. It is less clear, when research in the area of security began; even for ICT security this is unclear. One could claim, that security research started thousands of years ago, when the original Trojan Horse was designed. While one can probably find even earlier references to research on security issues, referring to the Trojan Horse can also take its justification from the fact, that the original Trojan Horse lead to a decisive end of a security issue after about 10 years. In any case it illustrates, that already several millennia of thinking (or not-thinking) were spent on the issue. Therefore this text starts with a description of relevant goals (1) as well as technical and other trends (2). Then (3) relevant instruments for ICT security are derived from the goals and trends. These instruments are not necessarily new but important for research due to their relevance in general or due to their high number of relevant open questions.

1 Goals

Two general goals seem to be of particular relevance for security research:

1. Multilateral Security, as it aims for a fair distribution of security among stakeholders, avoiding, that the security of some stakeholders dominates that of others.
2. The privacy compatibility of ICT security measures, as many security measures tend to become an unnecessary privacy threat for some stakeholders.

1.1 Multilateral Security

Multilateral Security [1, 2] aims at a balance between the competing security requirements of different parties. It means taking into consideration the security requirements of all parties involved. It also means considering all involved parties as potential attackers, as one cannot expect the various parties to trust each other. The "ideal" of Multilateral Security can be described as follows:

1. Considering Conflicts:

    1. Different parties involved in a system may have different, perhaps conflicting interests and security goals.

W. Jonker and M. Petković (Eds.): SDM 2013, LNCS 8425, pp. 28–32, 2014.
DOI: 10.1007/978-3-319-06811-4_6, © Springer International Publishing Switzerland 2014

2. Respecting Interests:

   1. Parties can specify their own interests and security goals.
   2. Conflicts can be recognized and negotiated.
   3. Negotiated results can be reliably enforced.

3. Supporting Sovereignty:

   1. Each party is only minimally required to place trust in the honesty of others.
   2. Each party is only minimally required to place trust in the technology of others.

Multilateral Security in general refers to all security goals, i.e. confidentiality, integrity, availability, or accountability can be in the interest of one party, but not necessarily in that of another. However a typical conflict occurs between the wish for privacy and the interest in cooperation. On one hand parties wish to protect their own sphere, information, and assets, on the other hand they strive for cooperation and wish to establish trust with partners, transfer values, or enable enforcement of agreements. To make Multilateral Security an effective protection of the weaker stakeholders it needs to go hand in hand with user enablement and especially with real choice from alternatives.

1.2 Privacy Compatibility of ICT Security Measures

ICT security measures or mechanisms can be in line with privacy goals, e.g. in access control, when confidentiality and privacy protection are closely related. However security mechanisms can also have a negative effect on privacy, e.g. when audit logs create additional data that can tell a lot of sensitive things about people and their interest. In general ICT security measures often trigger more and more data collections that need to be analysed for their impacts on privacy and possible alternatives.

2 Technical and Other Trends

ICT and related services are coming ever closer to people under paradigms like mobility, ubiquity, and personalization. These paradigms are also triggering the creation of more and more data about users, e.g. movement profiles. At the same times attacks by large state organisations on security and privacy protection of ICT services and infrastructures of all kind are now discussed more openly, especially since the recent disclosures of the USA NSA spying activities.

For some experts the revelations were no news, but for many people the dangers of undetected surveillance and manipulation of information are now becoming so obvious, that their trust into ICT infrastructures and their operators is massively reduced at least for some time. This may result in more support for thorough research addressing some fundamental weaknesses in current ICT architectures, e.g. the difficulties to control information flows. It also motivates the quest for infrastructures that are independent from overly swift government actions by storing less data or by being distributed wisely. In any case the relation between trust and security needs to be researched more thoroughly. Depending on the definition trust has at least two distinct meanings:

1. Trust can be seen as a consequence of security and assurance as e.g. the security certification paradigms see it: More perceived security and more endeavours to assure security lead to more trust.
2. Trust can be seen as a consequence of insecurity, as often done in social sciences: Trust is then the more or less rational belief in an acceptable outcome of an insecure situation. Therefore trust is dependent from insecurity or a lack of security: If there is security there is no basis for trust, as there is no insecure situation.

While these two distinct meanings of trust and their consequence for ICT security research seem to be reasonable understood, there are open questions with regard to the middle ground between them. More research seems to be needed on the cases where people have some trust or partial trust, e.g. only in parts of the ICT they use or only with regard to some aspects of security and privacy. These combinations of trust are conceptually difficult to grasp. Nevertheless they are very relevant, as in most real-life situations trust and distrust co-exist - most ICT products and services reach their (potential) users as combinations of several elements and involved parties. While some users may trust some ICT elements and involved parties, the same or other users may not be able to judge on the trustworthiness of other ICT elements and involved parties or even consider those as untrustworthy.

3 Instruments

3.1 Data Thriftiness

A number of research areas can be seen under the umbrella of data thriftiness. They are not completely new, but they need (more) research attention in order to further progress them to a status, that allows more usage in practical applications.

1. Partial Identities and Identifiers: More and more public and private parties are trying to overcome the natural borders between domains of data, making users ever more transparent from ever more perspectives. Partial identities and identifiers become more and more important for users to protect themselves by reducing the dangers of unwanted information flows.
2. Minimal Disclosure: Still much more personal information than needed is asked from users, e.g. for authorising them to use Internet resources. Risk management processes compatible with the minimal disclosure need to be established. One important building block for minimal disclosure is represented by Attribute Based Credentials [3], as they allow users to calibrate the amount of information they want to disclose.

3.2   Stability of Services and Reliability with Regard to Planning of Changes

Often Internet based services like Facebook change their features and their security and privacy default settings very fast and surprisingly. So their users have almost no chance to react and to protect their assets, e.g. to enact access control for a new feature that would publish data that was not accessible before. To enable innovation but to give people a realistic chance to react, proper plans for the establishment and communication of changes are needed. These plans need to be researched to balance innovation and new versions of software or services against the need for stability of users' environment.

3.3   Trustworthy Mobile Platforms and App-Ecosystems

Smartphones could be a great platform for credentials and other personal assets, but their operating systems and applications have so many security and privacy weaknesses, that many users don't dare to consider them trustworthy (in the first sense), even though they use them. For these mobile platforms more research is needed to enable technologies and architectures that European democratic governments can understand well enough to give a realistic assessment whether their citizen's data and cyber activities are protected appropriately. An approach to overcome the app-side of the problem (e.g. apps that leak their users' personal data to their developers or elsewhere) is to enhance the app ecosystem (e.g. the app-markets). App markets are to provide useful privacy information about individual apps in all the phases of apps' life cycle, but especially during app discovery, installation, and usage. Crowdsourcing may be used to protect against privacy-invasiveness of apps by influencing the rankings in (alternative) app-markets.

3.4   Strong Sovereign Assurance Tokens and Wallets

Assurance tokens (e.g. authorisation certificates) tend to contain more and more sensitive information, e.g. birth dates or authorizations for specific services or activities. Therefore they need special protection against undue transmission and exploitation. This protection can be provided either directly or via digital wallets. Examples are advanced smart cards or mobile devices with trustworthy secure elements that enable their holder to influence the character and degree of identification and the type of identification information. These devices are also to enable meaningful communication between the assurance token holder and the assurance token. Last but not least assurance tokens and wallets must be able to protect themselves. For example they need to be able to verify their respective controllers (readers) by e.g. an extra communication channel. Therefore a portfolio of communication mechanisms is needed, also to provide some redundancy. Moreover an independent clock, a sufficiently powerful access control mechanism to protect relevant data, and enough processing power for complex (crypto) operations are needed.

3.5   Trustworthy and Transparent ICT Infrastructures in General

Current ICT infrastructures are in general not really trustworthy. They lack technology and processes that European democratic governments can understand well enough to protect European citizens and businesses against e.g. espionage, manipulation, or domination by major players. An important special area is that of eID infrastructures, as they are used in many applications, another one is that of cloud computing services for SMEs, as SMEs are usually small against their cloud computing providers and therefore in a relatively weak position. In general more transparency of ICT infrastructures and the ICT used in them is needed. This needs to include open and frank descriptions, explanations, and discussions of current and future weaknesses, e.g. on the steps that have been taken to prevent illegitimate exploitation, and a pause, while the implications of the weaknesses become better understood. It also needs an infrastructure of independent institutions to assess the security and reliability of complex ICT [4].

Acknowledgement. André Deuker, Markus Tschersich, and Christian Weber provided valuable feedback to a draft version of this paper.

References

1. Rannenberg, K.: Recent development in information technology security evaluation – the need for evaluation criteria for multilateral security. In: Sizer, R., Yngström, L., Kaspersen, H., Fischer-Hübner, S. (eds.) Security and Control of Information Technology in Society – Proceedings of the IFIP TC9/WG 9.6 Working Conference, Onboard M/S Ilich and ashore at St. Petersburg, Russia, 12–17 August 1993. North-Holland Publishers, Amsterdam (1994). ISBN 0-444-81831-6
2. Rannenberg, K.: Multilateral security - a concept and examples for balanced security. In: Proceedings of the 9th ACM New Security Paradigms Workshop 2000, 19–21 September 2000, pp. 151–162. ACM Press. ISBN: 1-58113-260-3
3. Attribute-Based Credentials for Trust (ABC4Trust): https://abc4trust.eu
4. International Federation for Information Processing: IFIP statement on intentional weakening of security and trust mechanisms in ICT and the internet by government agencies and other major actors. www.ifip.org/images/stories/ifip/public/Announcements/web%20ifip%20statement%20underminingsecuritytrust%20mechanisms%204%20.pdf (2014). Accessed 23 April 2014

"Technology Should Be Smarter Than This!": A Vision for Overcoming the Great Authentication Fatigue

M. Angela Sasse[✉]

Human-Centred Technology, Research Institute for Science of Cyber Security, Department of Computer Science, University College London, London, UK
a.sasse@cs.ucl.ac.uk

Abstract. Security researchers identified 15 years ago that passwords create too much of a burden on users. But despite much research activity on alternative authentication mechanisms, there has been very little change for users in practice, and the implications for individual and organisations productivity are now severe. I argue that - rather than looking for alternative 'front-end' solutions, we must re-think the nature of authentication: we must drastically reduce the number of explicit authentication events users have to participate in, and use advanced technologies to implicitly authenticate users, without disrupting their productive activity.

My disciplinary background is in usability, and for a decade, I worked to improve the usability of emerging Internet systems and services. My focus on security (and later privacy, trust and identity aspects) started because an industrial collaborator faced security help desk costs that were spiraling out of control, and asked me to figure out 'why these stupid users cannot remember their passwords'. The resulting study conducted in collaboration with Anne Adams 'Users Are Not the Enemy' [1] published in 1999, the same year as Whitten & Tygar's 'Why Johnny can't Encrypt'. The two papers mark laid the foundation for the research area now referred to as Usable Security. Over the past decade and a bit, this area has flourished: there are now several conferences and workshops dedicated to the area, and papers on this topic have been accepted to top-tier security and usability conferences alike.

But things have not improved for the average user out there. As Herley [3] put it, most security managers "value users' time at zero". To date, the cost of individual user time and effort spent to what is not their primary goal and activity has been largely hidden. The result, as an intense frustration among users about the burden of security, and the erosion of their personal productivity. Users are acutely aware of this, and stop complying when the friction between the security task and their primary task becomes too high. They introduce workarounds which compromise security, and/or reorganise their primary tasks to minimize their exposure to security [4]. In the context of an organisation, the organisation ultimately pays a high price: the cost of reduced individual and business activity productivity, and that of security breaches which occur as a result of non-compliance. To put it bluntly, most organisations' security at present is an expensive Swiss cheese – to borrow the analogy from the guru

W. Jonker and M. Petković (Eds.): SDM 2013, LNCS 8425, pp. 33–36, 2014.
DOI: 10.1007/978-3-319-06811-4_7, © Springer International Publishing Switzerland 2014

of safety research, it is riddled with holes that ever so often align and let the threat through. Unlike good Swiss cheese, the current state of operational security stinks.

Authentication provides a clear example for this. After the publication of "Users are Not The Enemy", we campaigned for changes to reduce the burden of authentication. We had some success: many organisations introduced single sign-on, and reduced the frequency with which passwords expire. But has been no serious attempt to grab the nettle of the password-based infrastructure that is deeply embedded in current systems. In the 2000s, technology (Bill Gates, Bruce Shneier) and usability (Jacob Nielsen) gurus both declared it a non-problem that would be resolved through the introduction of biometrics, which they assumed to be usable by default 'since users don't have to remember anything'. But a decade later, we found that the password burden was still weighing down individuals and organisations alike [6]: single sign-ons, more relaxed policies, and password managers such as LastPass may have reduced the burden somewhat, but the explosive growth in the number of devices, applications and services we use means users still have to manage dozens of passwords. The introduction of self-service re-sets and account recovery mechanisms has increased the burden further: helpdesks staffed by humans to assist other humans a were a visible cost that organisations swiftly moved on – replacing them with a technology-based self-service reminder and re-set mechanisms that create yet more items that users have to think up and remember. In a recent study [7] found additional impact created by "too much" authentication: staff logged in less frequently from home or when travelling, or stopped doing so altogether – meaning colleagues and customers had to wait for information or assistance, which in turn held up their work. Some refused to have a company-owned laptop, or returned it. We also found several examples where staff had identified a business opportunity, but did not pursue it because authentication policies or mechanisms would have to be changed, and they could not face the time and emotional effort that would require. We diagnosed a case of severe Authentication Fatigue, top on the list generated an 'Authentication Hate List':

1. Re- authentication to the same system (e.g. because of 15 min time-outs)
2. Length and complexity makes passwords hard to create, recall and enter – and different rules for different systems compound this)
3. Authenticating to infrequently used systems (hard to recall)
4. Password expiry (having to create a new password, interference with the old one, and you have to create 4 passwords a year for a system you only used twice in the same period)
5. Additional credentials for password re-set mechanism

As in previous studies, we found users had created workarounds – to cope with the most hated re-authentication, many users installed mouse-jiggler software to prevent time-outs. Which of, course they forget quite often when they actually do get up and leave their system unattended. So why are we still stuck with high-effort, productivity-zapping authentication mechanisms rendered ineffective by user workarounds? The password nettle is still there, and until we have the courage to grab and remove it, workable mechanisms are hard to realise. In an attempt to reduce the authentication burden, the organisation we studied offered fingerprint sensors to its staff; some used it, and said it was great on a day-to-day basis. But because the underlying authentication infrastructure and policies had not been changed, every 3 months, the underlying password expired – so they had to find the pieced of paper with the current password, change it, write the new one down, and then re-enrol their fingerprint against the current password. Biometrics have potential to reduce user burden, but do not deliver usability if simply used as an interface solution. Usable security research on authentication to date has largely focused 'user interface' solutions: pictures that are assumed to be more memorable, or password managers (which have been adopted by some users). In an age of ubiquitous computing, the cloud, and touch screen devices, we need to thinking more broadly and boldly: with cloud computing, even long and complex passwords can be attacked at relatively low cost. The majority of user interactions is now with touch screen devices, rather than keyboards – and entering password of any length and complexity takes at least 3 times longer than doing so on a standard keyboard.

If we use passwords at all, they have to be memorable and quick and easy to enter – that means using some form of 2 factor authentication is inevitable. Most organisations adopt 2 Factor authentication for security reasons, and opt for token-based authentication in form of special devices, smartcards, software tokens, or phones to send additional codes (as Google, for instance, does). But these solutions may, at first glance, offer an improvement in security, they create yet more burden on users, who have to remember to carry tokens, or wait for and enter further credentials. And remember to obtain a credential in advance when travelling somewhere without phone reception.

What we need is a shift from repeated explicit to implicit authentication: in an age where commercial companies are able to use the masses of data we emit to identify and profile us with what many think is a frightening degree of accuracy [8] it is bizarre that users' activity is constantly disrupted by systems insisting that we prove who we are. The 'wall of authentication' [7] users currently face is the legacy of old-style command-and-control, perimeter-based security thinking, where it was acceptable to create big obstacles to keep attackers out of systems, and make it almost as difficult for legitimate users to get in. That approach is not sustainable, and we hear users [in 7, but also a range of other studies we conducted shouting in collective frustration that "technology should be smarter than this!" And consumer-based parts of the industry are beginning to move – the FIDO alliance [9], which numbers Google and Paypal amongst its members, is the example of a framework that replaces passwords altogether. It shows how smarter use of the information we have on users – their devices, location, biometrics, patterns of use – can be leveraged to provide low-effort authentication. The final step is to shift towards implicit authentication: application of usability principles to leverage user activity on the primary task, rather than create an explicit, secondary security task – making security not entirely transparent, but making it "zero perceived effort".. Biometrics that have been developed to deliver high levels of accuracy (building on Roy Maxion's work keystroke recognition [11]) can recognise users from the way they type, touch – and perhaps even sing [12] or think [13] a simple knowledge-based credential – as part of their main activity to deliver 0 Effort, 1 Step, 2 Factor Authentication. I have to admit to having dismissed the authentication described in [12] and [13] as impractical in the past, but the emergence of low-cost smart technology such as the Emotiv helmet [14], developed to provide faster input for gaming, brings the idea of users 'thinking their password' and having it entered at the same time into the realm of the possible. Authentication is only one security mechanism that needs a radical re-think and re-design – users are suffering from outdated and unworkable access control mechanisms, slow and timewasting CAPTCHAs and incomprehensible security warnings. We need to start designing security that starts with protecting what users do and value.

References

1. Adams, A., Sasse, M.A.: Users are not the enemy. Commun. ACM **42**(12), 40–46 (1999)
2. Whitten, A., Tygar, J.D.: Why Johnny can't encrypt: a usability evaluation of PGP 5.0. In: Proceedings of the 8th Conference on USENIX Security Symposium - Volume 8 (SSYM'99), USENIX Association, Berkeley, CA, USA, vol. 8, pp. 14–14 (1999)
3. Herley, C.: So long, and no thanks for the externalities: the rational rejection of security advice by users. In: Proceedings of the 2009 Workshop on New Security Paradigms, pp. 133–144 (2009)
4. Beautement, A., Sasse, M.A., Wonham, M.: The compliance budget: managing security behaviour in organisations. In: NSPW'08: Proceedings of the 2008 Workshop on New Security Paradigms, pp. 47–58 (2008)
5. Reason, J.T.: The Human Contribution: Unsafe Acts, Accidents and Heroic Recoveries. Ashgate Publishing Ltd., Farnham (2008)
6. Inglesant, P.G., Sasse, M.A.: The true cost of unusable password policies: password use in the wild. In: Proceedings of the SIGCHI Conference on Human Factors in Computing Systems, pp. 383–392. ACM (2010)
7. Steves, M., Chisnell, D., Sasse, M.A., Krol K., Wald H.: Report: Authentication Diary Study, National Institute of Standards and Technology, Gaithersburg, MD, USA. NISTIR <Publication TBA> (2013)
8. Nikiforakis, N., Kapravelos, A., Joosen, W., Kruegel, C., Piessens, F., Vigna, G.: Cookieless monster: exploring the ecosystem of web-based device fingerprinting. In: IEEE Symposium on Security and Privacy (2013)
9. Kirlappos, I., Beautement, A., Sasse, M.A.: "Comply or Die" is dead: long live security-aware principal agents. In: Adams, A.A., Brenner, M., Smith, M. (eds.) FC 2013. LNCS, vol. 7862, pp. 70–82. Springer, Heidelberg (2013)
10. FIDO alliance. www.fidoalliance.org/
11. Killourhy, K.S., Maxion, R.A.: Comparing anomaly-detection algorithms for keystroke dynamics. In: IEEE/IFIP International Conference on Dependable Systems and Networks 2009, DSN'09, pp. 125–134. IEEE (2009)
12. Gibson, M., Renaud, K., Conrad, M., Maple, C.: Musipass: authenticating me softly with my song. In: Proceedings of the 2009 Workshop on New Security Paradigms, pp. 85–100. ACM (2009)
13. Thorpe, J., van Oorschot, P.C., Somayaji, A.: Pass-thoughts: authenticating with our minds. In: Proceedings of the 2005 Workshop on New Security Paradigms, pp. 45–56. ACM (2005)
14. www.emotiv.com/

Data Security and Privacy in 2025?

Matthias Schunter[✉]

Intel Labs, Darmstadt, Germany
schunter@acm.org

Abstract. Security research aims at reducing the risk and consequences of attacks on information technology. Based on the projection of current trends, this vision paper makes an attempt at identifying potential security research challenges for the next 10 years. Examples of identified challenges are the trend to have pervasive computing in tiny devices, to collect and analyze data from these devices and other sources, and to increase the connection between IT and physical systems.

1 Data Security and Privacy in 2025

Security research aims at reducing the risk and consequences of attacks on information technology. Based on the projection of current trends, this vision paper makes an attempt at identifying potential security research challenges for the next 10 years. Particular trends that we believe will have a substantial impact on IT security are:

Computing and Sensors Everywhere: The trend to connect computing devices including smartphones, tablets, and entertainment devices is expected to accelerate to include industrial equipment, vehicles, and wearables. Research cited by IBM predicts that "more than 22 billion web-connected devices by 2020 [...] will generate more than 2.5 quintillion bytes of new data every day." If the technical progress continues at the pace of the last 15 years, a 2025 mobile device would have the performance of a 70 GHz processor, 256 TB of storage, and the size of 3×7 mm at a price tag of $16 [10]. A likely consequence is that sensing will be ubiquitous. Personal devices permanently record ambient sounds, video, position, acceleration, and proximity to other objects and will interact with your vehicle, your appliances, and peers on a continuous basis and will be able provide real-time augmented reality to end-users [4].

The Power of Analytics: This huge amount of data contains valuable information and enables real-time intelligent interaction with individuals. Applications for personal use include driver assistance, decision support, or augmented reality where people can obtain real-time and localized information through devices such as Google Glass and personal assistants. Similarly, enterprises have only explored a small subset of potential usages of this information and its value. Security technology has not even started to leverage recent advances in analytics to assess and mitigate risks.

Cyber physical Systems: Besides sensing and analyzing, an important trend is the increased direct and automated control of the physical reality through actuators. Actuators include power grids controlling power consumers, intelligent transportation

W. Jonker and M. Petković (Eds.): SDM 2013, LNCS 8425, pp. 37–41, 2014.
DOI: 10.1007/978-3-319-06811-4_8, © Springer International Publishing Switzerland 2014

systems, management of cities, and control of home appliances. For instance, Wikipedia cites a prediction that 30 % of households will delegate selected tasks to intelligent robots in 2022.

What about Security and Privacy? The possibilities and the potential value acts as a strong incentive to maximize use of these technologies. On the downside, individuals may be tempted to accept the privacy loss for the convenience gained. The continued growth of complexity will ensure that most systems remain vulnerable. This in turn, may continue to encourage industrial espionage for increasing the competitiveness of nations and enterprises.

2   Emergency Research Challenges

Huge amounts of data strive to be used (and mis-used). The overarching research challenge resulting from the outlined trend is: "How can society benefit from these capabilities without suffering the negative consequences." This holds even more since security and privacy risks may lead to rejection and pushback while the abundance of vulnerabilities may constitute a risk that may be unacceptable to enterprises and society.

2.1   Sensing, Computing, and Actuators Everywhere

The key research challenge is how to integrate privacy and confidentiality controls into a scenario where sensors are pervasive and potential adversaries are powerful. The unlimited capability to sense and collect data allows computing devices to fully monitor and permanently record a given environment. They may learn the location and identity of persons and objects and record their behavior without restrictions. Consequences of these abilities are unprecedented privacy and confidentiality challenges. For instance sensors that can records all activities in a building could void confidentiality for affected enterprises, or cameras in all mobile devices provide sufficient information to record the movements and behaviors of each individual.

Important questions are how can individuals control the sensed data derived from them, how can enterprises control the data generated from its behavior, and how to generate insight in a way to protect privacy. While initial research (such as usage control) exists for controlling well-defined data streams, tackling the problem of privacy-aware sensing has not been resolved yet. Similarly, sensing systems that ensure that the insight does not trigger privacy concerns only exist for special circumstances such as video[1].

A second area of research is the scalability of security to billions of devices. Groundwork is the key- and security management of these devices without any human intervention under potentially adversarial conditions[2]. Related research includes multi-factor authentication of physical devices [5], intrinsic hardware identities such

---

[1] E.g. [11] describes surveillance cameras where persons are replaced by anonymised shapes at the source.

[2] Assume that each device requires 1 s of human intervention, then 1B of devices require 32 person-years.

as Physically Unclonable Functions, and end-user-managed security for mobile devices.

While protecting in-bound information is important, a second challenge is to ensure safety when controlling actuators that affect physical systems, in particular in safety-critical applications such as industrial control systems or automobiles. Again, adversaries may take over large portions of the infrastructure and a fail-safe mode of operation is often not available.[3]

2.2 End-to-End Data Confidentiality and Privacy

While securing sensors is difficult, a related challenge is how to protect data along its processing chain including the sensing end-nodes, edge devices providing network connections, aggregators, the cloud backend, and the network interconnections. Today's security mechanisms allow end-to-end protection of unmodified data streams (e.g., using authentication codes, encryption, or hardware security and usage control policies). How to allow data aggregation and analysis along this chain while keeping data confidential, proving the correctness of the results, and maintaining verifiable privacy are open problems. Research in this area includes multi-party computations [7], homomorphic encryption [6], or trusted computing. In particular for cloud computing, these challenges gain relevance due to the increasing insider threats. In order to protect against individual cloud insiders, separation of duty can help [2]. However, if collusions of insiders are expected, today's research results allow only cloud storage while distributing data across multiple clouds [1]. How to secure computation in the cloud against insiders is largely unsolved.

2.3 Failure-Resistant Design

We believe that vulnerabilities will continue to grow and the corresponding risks will continue to increase. In particular for targeted attacks, we believe that a general defense is largely impossible and therefore these attacks will continue to be successful and their number will continue to grow.

A resulting research challenge is failure-resistant design of security systems. Today, security mechanisms are designed with the assumption that they protect from given risks and that they usually do not fail. For targeted attacks, this assumption needs to be revisited. Surviving failures and successful attacks must receive more attention when designing individual security systems. The new challenge to address is "how to ensure that the damage of envisioned *successful* attacks is minimized?". Potential mechanisms to enhance the survivability of IT systems are the early erasure of data, multiple lines of defense, and hardware-based trust mechanisms as fallback that allow to re-establish the security of a system after a successful attack. Such fallback mechanisms are particularly important if systems are designed for a long

---

[3] For instance, in case of a fault (e.g., caused by an attack) in an automotive control system, the breaks may still slow down and stop the car while there is no fail-safe mode for the steering.

life-time (e.g., monitoring systems for public infrastructures). An area of research on long-term security are Post-Quantum Crypto schemes that provide security even if the mathematical assumptions underpinning today's cryptography are broken [3].

3   Conclusion

While the IT industry will continue to change at a rapid pace and attacks are getting more powerful, the positive news is that there already exists a vast amount of security and privacy research that can be used to address these new challenges. To some extent, translating research into usable real systems is one of the bigger challenges we face.

Besides addressing the research challenges that we have outlined, an interesting consequence of the emerging sensor/analytics/actuator trend is that we expect security research to undergo a paradigm shift from black/white or trusted/untrusted towards a more analytics-based approach where the trust in entities lies on a continuum between trusted and untrusted. Classes of failure and attacks will be tolerated in this approach. This approach to will integrate trust assessment mechanisms along with data analysis to assess data based on its trustworthiness while automatically disregarding suspected outliers, untrusted data points, and data resulting from attacks.

Acknowledgements. This position paper solely reflects a subjective opinion of the author. Nevertheless, it was formed based on valuable input by my team at the Intel Collaborative Research Center for Secure Computing and at Intel Labs. In particular Christian Wachsmann of TU Darmstadt provided feedback on drafts of this position paper.

References

1. Bessani, A.; Correia, M.; Quaresma, B.; André, F., Sousa, P.: DepSky: dependable and secure storage in a cloud-of-clouds. In: 6th ACM SIGOPS/EuroSys European Systems Conference (EuroSys'11). ACM (2011)
2. Bleikertz, S., Kurmus, A., Nagy, Z.A., Schunter, M.: Secure cloud maintenance: protecting workloads against insider attacks. In: Proceedings of the 7th ACM Symposium on Information, Computer and Communications Security (ASIACCS '12), pp. 83–84. ACM, New York (2012). doi:10.1145/2414456.2414505
3. Buchmann, J., May, A., Vollmer, U.: Perspectives for cryptographic long-term security. Commun. ACM **49**(9), 50–55 (2006)
4. Brandon, J.: Top 5 Tech Predictions for 2023. http://www.inc.com/john-brandon/top-5-tech-predictions-for-2025.html (2013). Accessed 31 May 2013
5. Danev, B., Zanetti, D., Capkun, S.: On physical-layer identification of wireless devices. ACM Comput. Surv. **45**(1), 1–29 (2012). doi:10.1145/2379776.2379782. Article 6
6. Gentry, C.: Fully homomorphic encryption using ideal lattices. In: The 41st ACM Symposium on Theory of Computing (STOC) (2009)
7. Goldreich, O., Micali, S., Wigderson, A.: How to play ANY mental game. In: Proceedings of the Nineteenth Annual ACM Conference on Theory of Computing, pp. 218–229. ACM Press (1987)

8. Krings, A.: Design for survivability: a tradeoff space. In: Proceedings of the 4th Annual Workshop on Cyber Security and Information Intelligence Research: Developing Strategies to Meet the Cyber Security and Information Intelligence Challenges Ahead (CSIIRW '08). ACM, New York (2008). doi:10.1145/1413140.1413154
9. Roman, R., Najera, P., Lopez, J.: Securing the internet of things. IEEE Computer **44**(9), 51–58 (2011). doi:10.1109/MC.2011.291
10. Schetting, R.: In your ear with intelligent super computers - by 2025. http://futuretimes.net (2013). Accessed 31 May 2013
11. Senior, A., Pankanti, S., Hampapur, A., Brown, L., Ying-Li, T., Ekin, A., Connell, J., Chiao-Fe, S., Max, L.: Enabling video privacy through computer vision. IEEE Secur. Priv. **3**(3), 50–57 (2005). doi:10.1109/MSP.2005.65

Towards a Risk-Based Approach to Achieving Data Confidentiality in Cloud Computing

Sharad Mehrotra[✉]

Department of Computer Science,
University of California, Irvine, CA 92701, USA
uci.sharadmehrotra@gmail.com

Abstract. With the advent of cloud computing, data and computation outsourcing is fast emerging as a dominant trend for both individual users for personal data management as well as for enterprises wishing to exploit the cloud to limit investment and costs in IT. A fundamental challenge that arises when entities outsource data is the "loss of control over data". The paper focuses on the privacy and confidentiality implications of loss of control. Techniques/mechanisms to ensure data confidentiality have been studied in the literature in the context of database as a service (DAS). The paper identifies new opportunities and challenges that arise in the context of the cloud. In particular, the paper advocates a risk-based approach to data security in the context of cloud computing.

1 Introduction

Fueled by advances in virtualization and high-speed networking, cloud computing is emerging as a dominant computing paradigm for the future. Cloud computing can roughly be summarized as "X as a service" where X could be a virtualized infrastructure (e.g., computing and/or storage), a platform (e.g., OS, programming language execution environment, databases, web servers), software applications (e.g., Google apps), a service, or a test environment, etc. A distinguishing aspect of cloud computing is the utility computing model (aka pay-as-you-go model) where users get billed for the computers, storage, or any resources based on their usage with no up-front costs of purchasing the hardware/software or of managing the IT infrastructure. The cloud provides an illusion of limitless resources that one can tap into in times of need, limited only by the amount one wishes to spend on renting the resources. Despite numerous benefits, organizations, especially those that deal with potentially sensitive data (e.g., business secrets, sensitive client information such as credit card and social security numbers, medical records), hesitate to embrace the cloud model completely. One of the main impediments is the sense of *"loss of control"* over ones' data wherein the end-users (clients) cannot restrict the access to potentially sensitive data by other entities, whether they are other tenants to the common cloud resources or privileged insiders

This work has been funded through NSF grants CNS 118127, CNS 1212943, and CNS 1059436.

W. Jonker and M. Petković (Eds.): SDM 2013, LNCS 8425, pp. 42–47, 2014.
DOI: 10.1007/978-3-319-06811-4_9, © Springer International Publishing Switzerland 2014

who have access to the cloud infrastructure. The key operative issue here is the notion of trust. Loss of control, in itself, is not as much of an issue if clients/users could fully trust the service provider. In a world where service providers could be located anywhere, under varying legal jurisdictions; where privacy and confidentiality of ones data is subject to policies and laws that are at best (or under some circumstances) ambiguous; where policy compliance is virtually impossible to check, and the threat of "insider attacks" is very real – trust is a difficult property to achieve. Loss of control over resources (by migrating to the cloud) coupled with lack of trust (in the service provider) poses numerous concerns about data integrity (will service provider serve my data correctly? Can my data get corrupted?), availability (will I have access to my data and service at any time?), security, privacy and confidentiality (will sensitive data remain confidential? Will my data be vulnerable to misuse - by other tenants and/or by service provider?). In this position paper, we focus on the privacy and confidentiality aspects of data processing in public cloud environments.

An obvious approach to achieving confidentiality is to appropriately encrypt data prior to storing it on the cloud. This way, data remains secure against various types of attacks, whether they be due to using shared systems & resources also accessible to others, insider attacks, or data mining attacks leading to information leakage. While encrypting data mitigates many of the confidentiality concerns, it poses a new challenge - how does one continue to process encrypted data in the cloud? The challenge of searching and data processing over encrypted data has been addressed extensively in the literature. Over the past few decades, numerous cryptographic approaches as well as information hiding techniques have been developed to support basic computations over encrypted data [1, 6, 8]. For instance, a variety of semantically secure searchable encryption techniques that can support various forms of keyword search as well as range searches have been proposed. Likewise, work in the area of **Database As a Service (DAS)** [7] has explored support for SQL style queries with selections/projections/joins etc. over encrypted data. When processing cannot continue on the encrypted domain, the data is transferred to the secure client, which then decrypts the data and continues the computation. The goal in such processing is to minimize the client side work, while simultaneously minimizing data exposure. For instance [5], outlined how an SQL query could be split to execute partly on the server and partly on the client to compute the final answer. Many such approaches offer sliding scale confidentiality wherein higher confidentiality can be achieved, albeit extra overheads. Significant progress has been made in designing solutions that offer viable approaches when the computation to be performed on encrypted data is suitably constrained.

2 Challenges and Opportunities Beyond DAS

While the techniques for query processing/search in mixed security environments developed in the literature to support the DAS model provide a solid foundation for addressing the confidentiality challenge in cloud computing, the cloud setting offers additional opportunities as well as additional challenges that have not been fully explored in the DAS literature:

- Unlike DAS, where the resources were assumed to be very limited on the client side, in the cloud setting organizations may actually possess significant resources that meets majority of their storage and query processing needs. For instance, in the cloud setting data may only be partially outsourced, e.g., only non-sensitive part of the data may be kept on the cloud. Also, it is only at peak query loads that the computation needs to be offloaded to the cloud. This has implications from the security perspective since much of the processing involving sensitive data can be performed at the private side, e.g., if query primarily touches sensitive data, it could be executed on the private side.
- In DAS, since the goal was to fully outsource the data and computation, the focus of the solutions was on devising mechanism to compute on the encrypted representation (even though such techniques may incur significant overhead). In contrast, in the cloud environments, since local machines may have significant computational capabilities, solutions that incur limited amount of data exposure of sensitive data (possibly at a significant performance gain) become attractive.
- While DAS work has primarily dealt with database query workload (and text search [1]), in a cloud setting, we may be interested in more general computation mechanisms (i.e. not only database workloads). For instance, map-reduce (MR) frameworks are used widely for large-scale data analysis in the cloud. We may, thus, be interested in secure execution of MR jobs in public clouds.
- Another challenge is that of autonomy of the cloud service providers. It is unlikely that autonomous providers will likely implement new security protocols and algorithms (specially given significant overheads associated with adding security and the restrictive nature of cryptographic security for a large number of practical purposes). For instance, it is difficult to imagine Google making changes to the underlying storage models, data access protocols and interfaces used by its application services (such as Google Drive, Picasa, etc.) such that users can store/search/process data in encrypted form. This calls for a new, robust and more flexible approach to implement privacy and confidentiality of data in cloud-based applications.

3   Risk Aware Data Processing in Clouds

Given that general solutions that offer complete security in cloud setting are unlikely to emerge in the near future, we promote a *risk-based approach* to practical security for such settings. Unlike traditional security approaches that attempt to eliminate the possibility of attacks, a risk-based approach, instead of preventing loss of sensitive data, attempts to limit/control the exposure of sensitive data on public cloud by controlling what data and computation is offloaded to the public cloud and how such data is represented. Different ways to steer data through the public and private machines may exhibit different levels of risks and expose a tradeoff between exposure risks and system specific quality metrics that measure the effectiveness of a cloud based solution. Given such a tradeoff, the goal of the risk aware computing changes from purely attempting to maximize the application specific metrics to that of achieving a balance between performance and sensitive data disclosure risks. Let us illustrate the concept of a risk-based solution using a couple of example cloud-based system scenarios.

As a first motivation, consider a **hybrid cloud** setting wherein an organization seamlessly integrates its in-house computing resources with public cloud services to construct a secure and economical data processing solution. A growing number of organizations have turned to such a hybrid cloud model [1, 2] since it offers flexibility on the tasks that can be offloaded to public clouds thereby offering the advantages of increased throughput, reduced operational costs while maintaining security. Consider a data management workload (i.e., a set of database queries) that the organization would like to execute periodically with some timing guarantees. The workload may be too large for a given private infrastructure and the option might be to shift some queries to the public side. There are multiple choices for data processing – either shift some queries (and the corresponding data needed for their processing) to the public side, or alternatively, one could use DAS style query operator implementation whereby the public and private sides split the task of query execution cooperatively. In either case, the data and computation needs to be distributed and different workload distributions offer different levels of exposure risks and benefits (e.g., task completion time). A risk-based approach would attempt to find a solution that optimizes the performance subject to constraints on exposure risks. Or alternatively, it may attempt to minimize the risk while ensuring certain performance guarantees. Our previous work [11] has explored such a tradeoff for a static workload consisting of Hive queries.

As another scenario, consider a system that empowers users with control over data they may store in existing (autonomous) cloud-based services such as Box, Google drive, Google Calendar, etc. There are many ways to realize such a system – for instance, in our implementation, which we refer to as CloudProtect [3], the system is implemented as an intermediary privacy middleware that sits between clients and service providers that intercepts the clients' http requests, transforms the request to suitably encrypt/decrypt[1] the data based on the user's confidentiality policies before forwarding the request to the service provider. Encrypting data, may interfere with the user's experience with the service – while requests such as create, retrieve, update, delete, share and even search can be performed over encrypted data, functions such as language translation (Google) picture printing (Shutterfly or Picasa) require data to be decrypted first. In such a case, CloudProtect executes an exception protocol that retrieves the data from the server, decrypts it, and stores the data in cleartext prior to forwarding the service request. While CloudProtect offers continued seamless availability of web services, if every user's request (or many of them) results in an exception, the user's experience will be seriously compromised due to significant overheads of exception handling. An ideal approach will adaptively choose a representation of data on the cloud side that strikes a balance between the risk of data exposure with the usability of the service (i.e., reducing number of exceptions raised in CloudProtect). Such an approach would ensure, for instance, that data at rest is

---

[1] Since web services follow a custom data model, CloudProtect uses a format preserving encryption [2, 3].

always encrypted while data frequently used by requests that cannot be executed over encrypted representation is left in cleartext form at the service provider.

4 Challenges that Lie Ahead

The examples above illustrate 2 scenarios where risk based approach could be adopted to strike a balance between system specific metrics (e.g., performance, usability, timeliness etc.) and confidentiality. Our work in Radicle Project (http://radicle.ics.uci. edu) has explored such an approach in a few example cloud computing settings – namely, splitting database query workloads in hybrid clouds, developing a secure map reduce (MR) execution environment (entitled SEMROD) that controls the data exposure in multi-phase MR jobs, and CloudProtect middleware that empowers users control over data exposed in Web applications. While these systems make a strong case for a risk-based approach for data confidentiality in the cloud setting, much work lies ahead before a risk-based approach can become an effective tool in the arsenal for securing data in the cloud. First, and foremost, we need to develop appropriate metrics to model risks in cloud setting. One can use simple metrics such as number of sensitive data items exposed, and/or duration of the exposure, as a way of measuring risks (as is done in our prior work). Risks, however, depend upon a variety of factors – e.g., the vulnerability of the cloud infrastructure and steps the cloud provider has taken to secure the infrastructure, the adversaries and the nature of the attacks, on the degree of harm an adversary can cause to the data owner due to exposure, and the representation of the data on public clouds, to name a few. A risk-based approach requires proper models and metrics to quantify risks. Risk-based approaches expose tradeoffs between security and system specific properties (e.g., performance, usability, etc.) requiring users to make a choice. A natural question is how should the risks be communicated to the user and what kind of tools can be built to empower users to make an informed choice? Possible approaches based on HCI principles, social science research on risk communications, as well as, machine learning methods to learn user's tolerances to risk could be employed. Finally, another related challenge in developing a risk-based approach is in postulating the choice of data representation on the public cloud as a multi-criteria optimization. Such a formulation requires reasonable estimate of how the system will be used in the future (e.g., what requests will a user make to cloud services in the CloudProtect context, or what analysis tasks will the user execute in the hybrid cloud setting, etc.). This requires mechanisms for future workload predictions. Work on autonomic computing for workload prediction (usually done in the context of performance optimization, e.g., to determine what indices to create in a relational database) could possibly be exploited for such a task.

5 Concluding Remarks

Overall we believe that until efficient general computation over encrypted data representation is fully solved (unlikely in the near future), a risk-based approach sketched above provides a viable complementary mechanism to achieve practical security and data confidentiality in cloud computing setting. Such an approach can, of course, benefit from the ongoing work on cryptographic techniques that extend the nature/ types of computations one can perform over encrypted data.

References

1. Bagherzandi, A., Hore, B., Mehrotra, S.: Search over encrypted data. In: van Tilborg, H.C.A., Jajodia, S. (eds.) Encyclopedia of Cryptography and Security, pp. 1088–1093. Springer, New York (2011)
2. Bellare, M., Ristenpart, T., Rogaway, P., Stegers, T.: Format-Preserving Encryption, Cryptology ePrint Archive, Report 2009/251. http://eprint.iacr.org
3. Diallo, M.H., Hore, B., Chang, E.-C., Mehrotra, S., Venkatasubramanian, N.: CloudProtect: managing data privacy in cloud applications. In: 2012 IEEE Fifth International Conference on Cloud Computing, CLOUD, pp. 303–310 (2012)
4. Hybrid Cloud. The NIST Definition of Cloud Computing. National Institute of Science and Technology, Special, Publication, pp. 800–145 (2011)
5. Hacigümüs, H., Iyer, B.R., Li, C., Mehrotra, S.: Executing SQL over encrypted data in the database-service-provider model. In: SIGMOD, pp. 216–227 (2002)
6. Hacigumus, H., Hore, B., Mehrotra, S.: Privacy of outsourced data. In: van Tilborg, H.C.A., Jajodia, S. (eds.) Encyclopedia of Cryptography and Security, pp. 965–969. Springer, New York (2011)
7. Hacigumus, H., Iyer, B., Mehrotra, S.: Providing database as a service. In: IEEE International Conference in Data Engineering (2002)
8. Hore, B., Mehrotra, S., Hacigmus, H.: Managing and querying encrypted data. In: Gertz, M., Jajodia, S. (eds.) Handbook of Database Security, pp. 163–190. Springer, New York (2008)
9. Lev-Ram, M.: Why Zynga loves the hybrid cloud. http://techfortune.cnn.com/2012/04/09/ zynga-2/?iid=HP_LN (2012)
10. Mearian, L.: EMC's Tucci sees hybrid cloud becoming de facto standard. http://www. computerworld.com/s/article/9216573/EMC_s_Tucci_sees_hybrid_cloud_becoming_de_ facto_standard (2011)
11. Oktay, K.Y., Khadilkar, V., Hore, B., Kantarcioglu, M., Mehrotra, S., Thuraisingham, B.: Risk-aware workload distribution in hybrid clouds. In: IEEE CLOUD, pp. 229–236 (2012)

Internet of Things
Security, Privacy and Trust Considerations

Antonio Skarmeta and M. Victoria Moreno[✉]

Department of Information and Communications Engineering
Computer Science Faculty, University of Murcia, Murcia, Spain
{skarmeta,mvmoreno}@um.es

Abstract. Secure and reliable Internet of Things (IoT) presents the main challenges to face for sustainable and efficient IoT ecosystems based on privacy-aware systems. In this paper we present a concise description of such challenges.

Keywords: Internet of Things · Security · Privacy · Trust

1 Introduction

The extension of the Internet to smart things is estimated for reaching by 2020 between 50 and 100 billion of devices [1], defining the called Internet of Things (IoT) [2]. In not-so futuristic world of IoT, **security**, **privacy**, and **trust** need to be considered as fundamental design parameters (e.g. privacy-by-design) of sensor systems, because serious and multi-dimensional problems related with these areas are inherent to the IoT paradigm.

Internet of Things represents a key enabler for the *smartness* of a city, enabling the interaction between smart things and an effective integration of real world information and knowledge into the digital world. Smart (mobile) things instrumented with sensing and interaction capabilities or identification technologies such as RFID, will provide the means to capture information about the real world in much more detail as ever before, which means to influence real world entities and other actors of a smart city eco-system in real time. Therefore, IoT will be an essential part of the knowledge society and will provide new information-based business.

Nevertheless, the usage of IoT at large-scale creates the need to address adequately trust and privacy functions. In a world becoming more and more digital, security and privacy are going to be the key needs in the deployments of new applications, since citizens will only accept such deployments, if they really trust the devices and applications that they use and with which they interact. Thus, for livable cities it is needed to rely on secure and privacy-aware IoT infrastructures.

This work has been sponsored by European Commission through the FP7-SMARTIE-609062 and the FP7-SOCIOTAL-609112 EU Projects.

W. Jonker and M. Petković (Eds.): SDM 2013, LNCS 8425, pp. 48–53, 2014.
DOI: 10.1007/978-3-319-06811-4_10, © Springer International Publishing Switzerland 2014

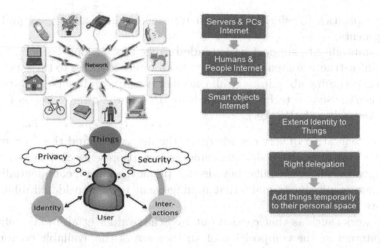

Fig. 1. Scenario where user security, privacy and trust need to be provided

Secure and trust considerations able infrastructures will form the backbone framework for public services, enterprises, and citizens to manage, control, optimize, and improve all operational aspects of their lives. In that sense, it is needed to evolve from a vision of sensors to an integrated view of smart objects forming part of our personal space, and as being shared, borrowed and, in general, having temporal associations with the users and their personal identity, while these aspects are addressed considering security and privacy rules. Figure 1 shows an example of scenario where user security, privacy and trust need to be provided.

In order to reach this vision, there are several research aspects to be undertaken along next years. These are:

- Authentication of sensors as proof of origin.
- Authentication of request for the access control to sensor data/configuration.
- Encryption, privacy, anti-eavesdropping, etc.
- Secure point to point connection for data integrity.
- Attribute based on control mechanisms.
- Techniques to support privacy-by-design issues, including data minimization, identification, authentication and anonymity.
- Fine-grain and self-configuring access control mechanisms emulating the real world.
- A fundamental building block for identity management, not only for the users' identities, but also for the things themselves.

Below, we describe some of the security and privacy approaches to provide new frameworks for security and privacy management of smart objects.

2   Operational Security in Internet of Things

As already mentioned, the number and diversity of sensors and devices deployed is growing tremendously, and this is due mainly thanks to:

- Their capacities to offer low cost air-interfaces which allow easy and quick deployments.
- Their suitability to support an extended range of solutions.
- Their infrastructure capacities to provide an Internet access to these networks, which is becoming ubiquitous to all the environments and users, and accessible for sensors based on technologies such as IPv6 Low Power Wireless Personal Area Networks (6LoWPAN).

A new generation of services where all the devices around the user are connected and providing sensed data will emerge fast. It presents challenges not only for management and scalability, but also for privacy, security, confidentiality and trust. These requirements make that management to be considered inherent to the Future Internet.

Some works such as that carried out by Schonwalder et al. in [3], define the Future Internet as the composition of an increase of the available content, the definition of new services centralized and personalized to the user, as well as an increase of the management. Thus, the management requirement is clearly a relevant challenge to cope. But this concern cannot be addressed through traditional approaches such as out-of-band and centralized management, which are usually considered, designed and definitively added to the service in a final stage of the solution development. In this new context, it is required a definition of the management issues at the design level, since a higher level of discussion and considerations is needed to solve the requirements of scalability and security, which present the need of manage millions of devices. Therefore, out-of-band management is not able to setup so large number of devices, and in contrast of this, an in-band management, with semi-automatic configuration, bootstrapping online, assisted deployment of keys, i.e. key management protocols, and device authentication based on identity instead of simple identifiers must be proposed to deal with all the challenges mentioned. Furthermore, the solutions which address all these features need to reach a self-management approach.

In conclusion, Future IoT requests new moderation and management services. For that reason, it is important to focus on offering a scalable and secure management protocol, which allows, on the one hand, the identity verification and authentication of the new devices deployed in a network, and, on the other hand, the extension of the trust domain to these new devices. Thereby, with this semi-automatic bootstrapping and configuration of new devices is more feasible, scalable and extensible the deployments based on IoT, and this protocol will be able to address the requirements from novel services proposed, where security will be highly required and desirable.

3   Security for Constrained Devices

Providing security, privacy and trust in embedded systems and pervasive sensor devices raises important technological challenges as the time-and resource-consuming cryptographic primitives, and security protocols are hard to realize in sensor devices and embedded platforms of merger resources. Since computing systems of sensor devices are, by their natures, extremely resource-constrained in terms of computing and communication capabilities, energy, power, chip and memory area, the challenge necessitates a deep and all-encompassing expertise in applied cryptography and security engineering. Moreover, the sensors generally have to work in harsh, uncontrolled, and even hostile surrounding conditions, where they are prone to attacks, misuse and malicious intentions.

To address the abovementioned issues and challenges, works would need to focus on the following three major areas:

1. Design of lightweight security protocols and cryptographic algorithms.
2. Lightweight and efficient implementations of security protocols and cryptographic algorithms.
3. Secure implementations in hardware and/or software.

For cryptographic algorithms, new standard based on hash functions [4], elliptic curve cryptography [5], and pairing-based cryptography are being considered, as well as the new hardware and/or software implementations of them. For security protocols, a special emphasis on anonymous group signature algorithms that will give way to efficient privacy-enhanced security and authentication schemes [6,7] are placed, where accountability is also provided. Specially, controlled-link ability [8], which allows tracking when there is an attack or malicious behaviour, is a challenging topic for which lightweight solutions are needed to be proposed.

4 Sharing Data in a Privacy-Preserving Way

To the large extent, IoT data may be of personal nature, therefore it is important to protect from unauthorised entities trying to access them. Data privacy is one of the most sensitive subjects in any discussion related with the topic of IoT protection [9].

The amount of data generated by IoT will be huge. In most cases, single pieces of information, i.e. single measurements, may not represent a significant threat for the owners of IoT devices (like temperature at a location, even heart rate of a person at a given moment). However, given that these devices will be generating data continuously, it is obvious that unauthorized access to such wealth of data can cause important problems, even it can harm the owners of the data (and possibly others, depending on the context of such data). Therefore, it is of paramount importance to protect the access to IoT data. On the other hand, some of the powers of IoT lie in the ability to share data, combine different inputs, process them and create additional values. Hence, it is equally important to enable access to data generated by other IoT devices, but as long as the use of such data in un-authorized or undesired ways is prevented.

The existing initiatives such as FI-WARE[1], address the privacy within the Optional Security Service Enabler[2], where privacy issue is concerned with authorization and authentication mechanisms. This includes a policy language to define what attributes (roles, identity, etc.) and credentials are requested to grant access to resources. It also includes a (data handling) policy language that defines how the requested data (attributes and credentials) are handled, and to whom they are passed on, providing the means to release and verify such attributes and credentials.

Finally, it is also important to consider the mechanisms enabling the protection of information based on encryption algorithms within the secure storage. In terms of the privacy policy implementation, one of the viable solutions is privacy-by-design, in which users would have the tools needed to manage their own data [10]. The fundamental privacy mechanisms lie in intelligent data management so that only the required data are collected. Detecting the redundancy, data are anonymised at the earliest possible stage and then deleted at the earliest convenience. Furthermore, the processing of the data gathered will have to be minimised according to a strict set of rules so that it cannot be re-used. There are already some approaches which focus on defining such methodology together with the mechanisms for the secure storage based on efficient cryptographic algorithms suited for resource constrained environments.

5 Conclusions

Internet of the Future will be a cluster of heterogeneous current and future infrastructures (networks, services, data, virtual entities, etc.) and of usages with mainly decentralized security and trust functions. According to all mentioned so far, it is remarkable that the emergence of sensing and actuating devices, the proliferation of user-generated content and nascent (Internet-only) services delivery create the need to address adequately trust and security aspects. Therefore, IoT brings new challenges regarding security and, in consequence, also for privacy, trust and reliability.

To conclude this article, below we summarize the major issues which will need to be addressed in short term for achieving sustainable and effective IoT systems:

- Design of a scalable management and bootstrapping protocol, and provide lightweight security protocols.
- Many devices are no longer protected by well-known mechanisms such as firewalls because they can be attacked via the wireless channel directly. In addition, devices can be stolen and analyzed by attackers to reveal their key material.

---

[1] FI-WARE Platform
http://forge.fi-ware.eu/plugins/mediawiki/wiki/fiware/index.php.
[2] FI-WARE Security
http://forge.fi-ware.eu/plugins/mediawiki/wiki/fiware/index.php/
FI-WARE_Security#Optional_Security_Service_Enabler.

- Combining data from different sources is the other major issue since there is no trust relationship between data providers and data consumers, at least not from the very beginning.
- Secure data exchange is required between IoT devices and consumers of their information.
- Architectures need to provide security and privacy features through dynamic trust models.
- Security and credential management need to be adapted to IoT restrictions.
- Future Internet architectures need to consider IoT security and privacy as first class objects.

References

1. Sundmaeker, H., Guillemin, P., Friess, P., Woelffl, S.: Vision and challenges for realising the Internet of Things. Cluster of European Research Projects on the Internet of Things (CERP-IoT) (2010)
2. Atzori, L., Iera, A., Morabito, G.: The internet of things: a survey. Comput. Netw. **54**(15), 2787–2805 (2010)
3. Schonwalder, J., Fouquet, M., Rodosek, G., Hochstatter, I.: Future internet= content+ services+ management. IEEE Commun. Mag. **47**(7), 27–33 (2009)
4. Akin, A., Aysu, A., Ulusel, O.C., Savas, E.: Efficient hardware implementations of high throughput SHA-3 candidates keccak, luffa and blue midnight wish for single- and multi-message hashing. In: Proceedings of the 3rd International Conference on Security of Information and Networks, pp. 168–177. ACM (2010)
5. Öztürk, E., Sunar, B., Savaş, E.: Low-power elliptic curve cryptography using scaled modular arithmetic. In: Joye, M., Quisquater, J.-J. (eds.) CHES 2004. LNCS, vol. 3156, pp. 92–106. Springer, Heidelberg (2004)
6. Ren, K., Lou, W.: A sophisticated privacy-enhanced yet accountable security framework for metropolitan wireless mesh networks. In: The 28th International Conference on Distributed Computing Systems. ICDCS'08, pp. 286–294. IEEE (2008)
7. Durahim, A.O., Savas, E.: A2-MAKE: an efficient anonymous and accountable mutual authentication and key agreement protocol for WMNs. Ad Hoc Netw. **9**(7), 1202–1220 (2011)
8. Hwang, J.Y., Lee, S., Chung, B.H., Cho, H.S., Nyang, D.: Short group signatures with controllable linkability. In: 2011 Workshop on Lightweight Security and Privacy: Devices, Protocols and Applications (LightSec), pp. 44–52. IEEE (2011)
9. Roman, R., Najera, P., Lopez, J.: Securing the Internet of Things. Computer **44**(9), 51–58 (2011)
10. Gudymenko, I., Borcea-Pfitzmann, K., Tietze, K.: Privacy implications of the Internet of Things. In: Wichert, R., Van Laerhoven, K., Gelissen, J. (eds.) AmI 2011. CCIS, vol. 277, pp. 280–286. Springer, Heidelberg (2012)

Security, Privacy and Trust: From Innovation Blocker to Innovation Enabler

Willem Jonker[3] and Milan Petković[1,2(✉)]

[1] Philips Research Europe, High Tech Campus, Eindhoven, The Netherlands
[2] Eindhoven University of Technology, Eindhoven, The Netherlands
milan.petkovic@philips.com
[3] EIT ICT Labs, Brussels, Belgium

Abstract. This paper reflects on security, privacy and trust from the point of you of the innovation in information and communication technologies. It also considers social, economic and legal aspects that need to be taken into account in the development cycles of new technologies. Finally, the major research challenges, which need to be overcome to ensure the future of the digital world, protect people privacy and enable even more rapid innovation, have been discussed.

Keywords: Security · Privacy and trust

1 Introduction

Information and Communication Technology (ICT) is one of the most disruptive technologies of our time and as a driver of economic growth and quality of life, omnipresent in today's society. ICT is characterized by ever shorter technology cycles, which require continuous adaption of systems and processes. The high dependence on fast evolving ICT poses serious challenges when it comes to dependability as well as social acceptance.

The current developments of high speed (mobile) networks enable rapid and instantaneous sharing of information between almost any places on the globe. People that are on-line can be traced continuously and the fast deployment of sensor technology adds to that that even those off-line can be almost constantly observed. This combination of instant proliferation of information and continuous monitoring of behavior makes that people feel infringed in their personal life sphere.

Under the above conditions the interest in research in the area of Privacy and Trust is growing fast. Privacy and Trust require intrinsically a multidisciplinary approach, where social, economic, legal, and technical aspects have to be merged into integrated solutions. Unfortunately today this is very often not the case. Technical solutions are being presented that have no social or legal foundation and as a result are not being used. The social debate is often lacking technical foundation which results into myths and suspicion. And finally law has difficulties in keeping at pace with technical developments.

Unfortunately the security research community itself is sometimes fuelling fear and suspicion by pointing at security vulnerabilities without too much nuance.

W. Jonker and M. Petković (Eds.): SDM 2013, LNCS 8425, pp. 54–58, 2014.
DOI: 10.1007/978-3-319-06811-4_11, © Springer International Publishing Switzerland 2014

Laymen get easily confused and as a result public debates move into a direction that leads to blocking ICT innovations such as for example electronic health records, road pricing and electronic voting machines in the Netherlands, and many applications of RFID-tags and other sensors world-wide.

Dependability, and especially security, privacy and trust, become a serious challenge with the deep penetration of ICT in almost any (critical) infrastructure. Security issues related to the Internet are meanwhile well known by the general public due to the widespread of security attacks on the Web. The ICT dependency will only grow with developments like Cloud Computing and Cyber Physical Systems that connect embedded systems to the Web. Phones, cars, planes, factories, hospitals, etc. are becoming critically depended on ICT as can be seen in areas such as smart grids for energy generation and distribution, intelligent mobility solutions for urban traffic management, on-line voting for general elections and smart production as pursued in the German Industry 4.0 initiative.

In order to be effective in the development of high impact innovations addressing societal challenges that are sensitive in terms of privacy or trust, the design of such solutions should from the very beginning involve social, economic, technical and legal specialists that map out the potential privacy and trust issues in a multi-disciplinary threat model. Based on such a threat model not only the system design should be developed but also the social-legal-economic design to prepare a proper embedding in society. Such an approach where security and privacy considerations form an integral part of the overall solution design (security and privacy by design) will make that security and privacy concerns are the enablers of innovation rather than the blockers as is it often seen today.

2 Key ICT Drivers to Invade Privacy

There are three major ICT developments that are perceived by the general public as key enablers for the infringement of their privacy. The first is the development of omnipresent connectivity via fixed and mobile networks, which leads to a situation where people are almost always on-line and feel continuously monitored in the cyber world. The second is the development of sensor technologies that allows embedding of sensors in wide range of devices and environments which leads to a situation where people feel continuously monitored in the physical world. The third is the development of advanced data analytics, mining and profiling techniques that can operate on huge data sets which leads to a situation that people feel that based on their behavior in both the physical and cyber world their beliefs, values, and intentions can be determined by governments, different organizations and companies.

3 Social, Economic, and Legal Aspects

With respect to connectivity the initial social and legal attitude has been that digital networks replace physical distribution networks of documents and letters. So sending an email is the digital equivalent of sending a physical letter. And as a result the social expectation is that the content of an email will only and only be accessed by the receiver. The legal framework for emails is trying to catch up with this but is not adequate either in the regulation itself or the enforcement. Many incidents lead to a perception with the general public that sending an email is more like sending a letter to a newspaper than writing a confidential letter. Although not exactly the same issue, but closely related, is the debate about the exact legislation of net-neutrality, which again fuels the wide-spread distrust towards operators of telecommunication infrastructures. However today's networks are no longer simply supporting e-mails or phone calls, they have grown into complex data and communication infrastructures where all kind of information is exchange and stored (tweets, Facebook pages, Wikipedia pages, LinkedIn, WhatsApp messages etc.). As a result the social perception of what we call the World Wide Web or the cyber world is very diverse and far apart from a simple mirror of known concepts from the physical world.

With respect to sensors and monitoring, the social attitude has always been one of suspicion. At the same time there is an enormous increase of surveillance cameras for example. Although they did meet a lot of resistance at first, there is a growing acceptance and most people completely accept that they are continuously observed at airports, city centers, in shops, in stadia, during events, in railway stations, etc. Often the argument of public safety is enough for most people to give up their resistance.

With respect to data analytics, mining and profiling techniques that operate on huge data sets, the general public today has little notion of the strengths and limitation of these techniques which leads to distrust and myths. Economic models play an important role here, since no business can be sustained by providing web services to end-users for free. So other source of income such as targeted advertising is needed which in turn requires profiling of users (e.g. driving business models behind companies like Google and Facebook).

From a more general socio-economic-legal perspective the OECD [1] has since long listed a number of principles that should be guiding when it comes to the treatment of personal data, amongst which the Collection Limitation Principle (data should be obtained by lawful and fair means and, where appropriate, with the knowledge or consent of the data subject), Data Quality Principle (relevant to the purposes for which they are to be used, and, to the extent necessary for those purposes, should be accurate, complete and kept up-to-date), Purpose Specification Principle (specified not later than at the time of data collection and the subsequent use limited to the fulfillment of those purposes or such others as are not incompatible with those purposes and as are specified on each occasion of change of purpose), Use Limitation Principle (not be disclosed, made available or otherwise used for purposes other than those specified except with the consent of the data subject or by the authority of law), Accountability Principle (data controller should be accountable for complying). From a legislation and technical perspective quite some work needs to be done to establish a situation where the general public starts to trust that the OECD principles are really governing our modern communication and information infrastructures. After a lot of debates, new data protection regulation in Europe is on its way to be established.

4 Key Technologies Addressing Security, Privacy and Trust

Encryption is an established way of hiding information. A key challenge with encryption is to develop efficient techniques that are highly secure and at the same time can run on very small footprints such as for example sensors. Another key challenge is to develop practical encryption schemes (e.g. homomorphic schemes) that allow data operations in the encrypted domain[1] (e.g. data mining or search in encrypted data).

Access control is developing from a centralized approach with large databases shielded via access control managers towards access and usage control techniques for open environments that allow policy to travel with the data that needs to be protected based on enhanced encryption techniques (e.g. Attribute Based Encryption [2]). Policy enforcement with decentralized control in distributed environments and the Cloud with key management, change management, and revocation remain to be very challenging.

Authentication techniques are essential ingredients in making sure that the right subjects get access to the right information and communication. The trend is to move towards certificate based solutions, however the current complexity still makes these techniques hard to use and fairly easy to compromise due to poor implementations. Claim (attribute)-based, privacy-preserving authentication systems such as Idemix [3] and uProve [4] are also finding their place in the landscape[2]. Another trend is the coupling of physical and digital identities via biometrics. Although for specific applications fingerprints and iris scans are being deployed there is still a long way to go to improve accuracy and decrease false positives and have the general public accept large scale deployment of biometric identification technology. Dealing with identity fraud in an effective way is another key challenge here.

The concept of big data influences many information security fields too. Intrusion detection, data leakage detection and protection are gaining a lot of attention due to many security and privacy breaches happening worldwide resulting in significant monetary losses. The current data leakage detection technologies suffer from low accuracy rates and many false positives. New white-box approaches [5] that make sue of big data and data analytics can boost the applicability of scientific results in the practice.

Reputation management aims at establishing trust in subjects or organizations by soliciting in a transparent way experiences and making them public. Reputation systems can be very effective but are also vulnerable to all kinds of fraud especially in an open networked environment (for example amongst others the usefulness of reputation systems highly depends on trustworthy authentication).

For all these technologies holds that successful deployment is only possible if the technology development is done with a deep understanding of the social, economic

---

[1] See for example work on privacy-preserving data mining in the Trusted HealthCare Services (THeCS) project – http://security1.win.tue.nl/THeCS/publication.html.

[2] See for example the work done in the AU2EU project – www.au2eu.eu.

and legal context in which they will be used. At the same time the technological development should go hand in hand with the development of the legal-economic framework in order to arrive at social acceptance.

5 Conclusion

ICT driven innovations are often hampered by security and privacy concerns. The reason for this is a combination of social, economic, legal and technical factors. In order to drive ICT innovations for economic growth and quality of life it is of key importance that technological developments go hand in hand with the development of legal-economic frameworks in order to arrive at social acceptance.

Acknowledgments. This work has been partially funded by the EC via grant agreement no. 611659 for the AU2EU project, as well as by the Dutch national program COMMIT under the THeCS project.

References

1. OECD - Guidelines on the Protection of Privacy and Transborder Flows of Personal Data. http://www.oecd.org/internet/ieconomy/oecdguidelinesontheprotectionofprivacyandtransborder flowsofpersonaldata.htm
2. Sahai, A., Waters, B.: Fuzzy identity-based encryption. In: Cramer, R. (ed.) EUROCRYPT 2005. LNCS, vol. 3494, pp. 457–473. Springer, Heidelberg (2005)
3. Camenisch, J., Lehmann, A., Neven, G.: Electronic identities need private credentials. IEEE Secur. Priv. **10**(1), 80–83 (2012)
4. Paquin, C.: U-Prove Technology Overview V1.1 (Revision 2). Microsoft, Apr 2013
5. Costante, E., Vavilis, S., Etalle, S., den Hartog, J., Petkovic, M., Zannone, N.: Database Anomalous Activities - Detection and Quantification. SECRYPT 2013, pp. 603–608

Workshop Papers

Secure Similar Document Detection
with Simhash

Sahin Buyrukbilen[1] and Spiridon Bakiras[2]([✉])

[1] The Graduate Center, City University of New York, New York, USA
sbuyrukbilen@gc.cuny.edu
[2] John Jay College, City University of New York, New York, USA
sbakiras@jjay.cuny.edu

Abstract. Similar document detection is a well-studied problem with important application domains, such as plagiarism detection, document archiving, and patent/copyright protection. Recently, the research focus has shifted towards the privacy-preserving version of the problem, in which two parties want to identify similar documents within their respective datasets. These methods apply to scenarios such as patent protection or intelligence collaboration, where the contents of the documents at both parties should be kept secret. Nevertheless, existing protocols on secure similar document detection suffer from high computational and/or communication costs, which renders them impractical for large datasets. In this work, we introduce a solution based on *simhash* document fingerprints, which essentially reduce the problem to a secure XOR computation between two bit vectors. Our experimental results demonstrate that the proposed method improves the computational and communication costs by at least one order of magnitude compared to the current state-of-the-art protocol. Moreover, it achieves a high level of precision and recall.

1 Introduction

Similar document detection is an important problem in computing, and has attracted a lot of research interest since its introduction by Manber [10]. Specifically, with digital data production growing exponentially, efficient file system management has become crucial. Detecting similar files facilitates better indexing, and provides efficient access to the file system. Furthermore, it protects against security breaches by identifying file versions that are changed by a virus or a hacker. Similarly, web search engines periodically crawl the entire web to collect individual pages for indexing [11]. When a web page is already present in the index, its newer version may differ only in terms of a dynamic advertisement or a visitor counter and may, thus, be ignored. Therefore, detecting similar pages is of paramount importance for designing efficient web crawlers. Finally, plagiarism detection and copyright protection are two other major applications that are built upon similar document detection.

While plaintext similar document detection is extremely important, it is not sufficient for secure and private operations over sensitive data. In many cases,

W. Jonker and M. Petković (Eds.): SDM 2013, LNCS 8425, pp. 61–75, 2014.
DOI: 10.1007/978-3-319-06811-4_12, © Springer International Publishing Switzerland 2014

owners of sensitive data may be forced to share their datasets with the government or other entities, in order to comply with existing regulations. For example, health care companies may be asked to provide data to monitor certain diseases reported in their databases. This may be accomplished by identifying similar attribute patterns in patient diagnosis information from different entities. Obviously, such pattern searches cannot be performed without secure protocols, since they may lead to severe privacy violations for the individuals included in the various databases.

Data sharing for intelligence operations also involves risks when disclosing classified information to other parties. A person of interest may have records at several intelligence agencies under different names with similar attributes. To identify similar records, the participating agencies may only wish to disclose the existence of records akin to the query. Detecting violations of the academic double submission policy is another problem with similar restrictions. For example, a conference's organization committee may want to know whether the articles submitted to their conference are concurrently submitted to other publication venues. Since research articles are considered confidential until published, their contents cannot be revealed unless a similar article is found in another venue.

Secure similar document detection (SSDD) leverages secure two-party computation protocols, in order to solve the above problems that arise due to the distributed ownership of the data. In particular, SSDD involves two parties, each holding their own private dataset. Neither party wants to share their data in plaintext format, but they both agree to identify any similar documents within their respective databases. The objective is to compute the similarity scores between every pair of documents without revealing any additional information about their contents. In existing work, document similarity is computed with either the inner product of public key encrypted vectors [7,8,12] or with secure set intersection cardinality methods based on N-grams [1]. However, the computational cost of inner product based similarity is very high, due to numerous public key operations. On the other hand, N-gram based methods are more computationally efficient, but they incur a high communication cost as the number of documents increases.

In this study, we present a novel method based on *simhash* document fingerprints[1]. Simhash is essentially a dimensionality reduction technique that encodes all the document terms and their frequencies into a fixed-size bit vector (typically 64 bits). Unlike classical hashing algorithms that produce uniformly random digests, the simhash digests of two similar documents will only differ in a few bit positions [6]. This enables us to (i) evaluate the similarity over a fairly small data structure rather than large vectors, and (ii) reduce the similarity calculation to a secure XOR computation between two bit vectors. To further improve the privacy preserving properties of our approach, we modify the basic method to hide the similarity scores of the compared documents. In particular, the enhanced version of our protocol returns all the document pairs whose similarity is above a user-defined threshold, while maintaining the exact scores secret. This is the

---

[1] We follow the simhash definition of Charikar [2].

first protocol in the literature that provides this functionality. Our experimental results demonstrate that the proposed methods improve the computational and communication costs by at least one order of magnitude compared to the current state-of-the-art protocol. Moreover, they achieve a high level of precision and recall.

The remainder of the paper is organized as follows. Section 2 describes the various primitives utilized in our methods and summarizes previous work on secure similar document detection. Section 3 presents the formal definition of the SSDD query and describes the underlying threat model and security. Section 4 introduces the details of our basic protocol and Sect. 5 presents the enhanced version that hides the exact similarity scores. Section 6 illustrates the results of our experiments and Sect. 7 concludes our work.

2   Background

Section 2.1 introduces the cryptographic primitives utilized in our methods and Sect. 2.2 describes the simhash algorithm. Section 2.3 surveys the related work on secure similar document detection.

2.1   Cryptographic Primitives

Homomorphic Encryption. Homomorphism in encryption allows one to evaluate arithmetic operations, such as multiplication and addition, over plaintext values by manipulating their corresponding ciphertexts. Most public key encryption schemes in the literature are *partially* homomorphic, i.e., they allow the evaluation of only one type of operation (either addition or multiplication).

In our work, we utilize ElGamal's *additively* homomorphic encryption scheme [3,5]. The scheme incorporates key generation, encryption, and decryption algorithms, as shown in Fig. 1. The homomorphic properties of this cryptosystem are as follows (where $E(\cdot)$ denotes encryption):

$$E(m_1 + m_2) = E(m_1)E(m_2)$$

$$E(m_1 - m_2) = E(m_1)E(m_2)^{-1}$$

$$E(m_1 k) = E(m_1)^k$$

Note that, ElGamal's scheme is *semantically* secure, i.e., it is infeasible to derive any information about a plaintext, given its ciphertext and the public key that was used to encrypt it. Its security is based on the decisional Diffie-Hellman assumption. Also note that the decryption process involves a discrete logarithm computation. If the encrypted values are not too large (which is the case in our protocol) it is possible to precompute all possible results and use them as a lookup table to speed up the decryption process.

Secure Two-Party Computation. A secure two-party computation protocol [9] allows two parties, Alice and Bob, to jointly compute a function based on their

---

ElGamal cryptosystem

Key generation
1. Instantiate a cyclic group G of prime order p, with generator g (G, g, and p are public knowledge)
2. Choose a *private* key x, uniformly at random from $\mathbb{Z}_p^*$
3. Publish the *public* key $h = g^x$

Encryption
1. Let m be the private message
2. Choose r, uniformly at random from $\mathbb{Z}_p^*$
3. Compute ciphertext $(c_1, c_2) = (g^r, h^{r+m})$

Decryption
1. Compute $h^m = c_2 \cdot (c_1^x)^{-1}$
2. Solve the discrete logarithm to retrieve m

Fig. 1. The ElGamal cryptosystem

---

inputs, while maintaining their inputs secret (i.e., they only learn the function output). Yao's *garbled circuit* technique [14] is a generic two-party computation protocol that can evaluate securely any function, given its Boolean circuit representation. Nevertheless, Yao's technique is efficient only for relatively simple functions, i.e., when the number of input wires and logic gates is small. In particular, every input wire (for one of the parties) necessitates the execution of an Oblivious Transfer (OT) [13] protocol that is computationally expensive, while the total number of gates affects the overall communication and circuit construction/evaluation costs.

Besides Yao's generic protocol, researchers have also devised application dependent protocols that typically leverage the properties of additively homomorphic encryption. As an example, consider the *secure inner product* computation that is used extensively in previous work [8,12]. For simplicity, assume that Alice holds vector $\langle a_1, a_2 \rangle$ and Bob holds vector $\langle b_1, b_2 \rangle$. The objective is for Alice to securely compute $S = a_1 b_1 + a_2 b_2$. Initially, Alice encrypts her input with her public key and sends $E(a_1), E(a_2)$ to Bob. Next, Bob utilizes the properties of homomorphic encryption to produce $E(S) = E(a_1)^{b_1} E(a_2)^{b_2}$. Finally, Alice decrypts the result and learns the value of S.

2.2 Simhash

Simhash maps a high dimensional feature vector into a fixed-size bit string [2]. However, unlike classical hashing algorithms, simhash produces fingerprints that have a large number of matching bits when the underlying documents are similar. Computing the simhash fingerprint from a text document is a fairly simple process. First, one has to extract all the document terms along with their weights (e.g., how many times they appear in the document). Then, a vector of l counters $\langle c_0, c_1, \ldots, c_{l-1} \rangle$ is initialized, where l is the size of the simhash fingerprint (e.g., 64 bits). Each of the document's terms is then hashed with a standard hashing algorithm, such as SHA-1. If the bit at position i ($i \in \{0, 1, \ldots, l-1\}$) in the resulting SHA-1 digest is 0, c_i is decremented by the weight of that term; otherwise, c_i is incremented by the same weight. When all document terms are processed, the simhash fingerprint is constructed as follows: for all $i \in \{0, 1, \ldots, l-1\}$, if $c_i > 0$, set the corresponding bit to 1; otherwise, set the bit to 0.

2.3 Related Work

The problem of secure similar document detection was first introduced by Jiang et al. [7]. In their approach, Alice and Bob first run a secure protocol to identify the common terms that appear in both datasets (dictionary). Then, similarity is computed with the *cosine* of the angle between two document term vectors. The cosine computation requires a secure inner product protocol, identical to the one described in Sect. 2.1. Specifically, for Alice to compare a single document against Bob's database, she first uses her public key to encrypt the weights of every term in the dictionary (if the term does not exist in Alice's document, its weight is 0). After Bob receives the encrypted vector, he uses his plaintext term vectors to blindly compute the encryptions of the inner products for all documents. Finally, Alice decrypts the results and computes the similarity between her document and each document in Bob's database. This protocol is computationally expensive, because of numerous public key operations at both parties. Furthermore, its performance degrades as the size of the dictionary space increases. For example, the similarity search between two document sets, each containing 500 documents, takes about a week to complete [7].

The authors of [7] extend their work in [12] with two optimizations. First, to reduce the number of modular multiplications at Bob, they ignore every ciphertext in Alice's vector where the corresponding plaintext value at Bob is zero. Second, to reduce the number of document comparisons, each party applies (in a pre-processing step) a k-means clustering algorithm on their documents. The idea is to initially compare only the cluster representatives and measure their similarity. If that similarity value is above a certain threshold, then the documents in both clusters are compared in a pairwise manner. Nevertheless, the drawback of clustering is that it is sensitive to the value of k. If k does not accurately reflect the underlying document similarities, it may result in a significant loss in query precision and recall.

Jiang and Samanthula [8] propose the use of N-grams in their SSDD protocol. An N-gram representation of a document consists of all the document's substrings of size N (after removing all punctuation marks and whitespaces). In general, N-grams are considered a better document representation method than term vectors, because they are language independent, more sensitive to local similarity, simple, and less sensitive to document modifications [8]. Specifically, Jiang and Samanthula utilize 3-gram sets and define the similarity between two documents as the Jaccard index of their 3-gram sets. Prior to protocol execution, both parties create the 3-gram sets of their documents and Bob discloses his *global* 3-gram set to Alice. To compare a pair of documents, Alice and Bob create the binary vectors of the corresponding 3-gram sets with respect to Bob's global 3-gram set (let A be Alice's vector and B be Bob's vector). Next, the two parties invoke a secure two-party computation protocol to compute $|A \cap B|$ in an additively split form. Finally, they run a secure division protocol to compute the Jaccard index $J = \frac{|A \cap B|}{|A \cup B|}$. Unfortunately, the above protocol is not secure [1], because Bob has to reveal his global 3-gram set to Alice. By utilizing this information, Alice can easily check whether a word appears in Bob's global collection, which is an obvious security breach.

Blundo et al. [1] introduce EsPRESSo, a protocol for privacy-preserving evaluation of sample set similarity. It is based on the private set intersection cardinality (PSI-CA) protocol of De Cristafaro et al. [4]. The authors show that one possible application of EsPRESSo is similar document detection and propose a solution based on 3-grams. To compare two documents, Alice and Bob first create the 3-gram sets of their respective documents. Next, Alice hashes her 3-grams and raises the resulting digests to a random number R_a (let's call this set A). She then sends A to Bob who, in turn, raises these values to his random number R_b and randomly permutes the set. He also hashes his 3-gram set members and raises the hash values to R_b (let's call this set B). Bob then sends both sets back to Alice. Alice removes R_a from A and computes the cardinality of the intersection between A and B ($|A \cap B|$). From this value, she computes the Jaccard index as $J = \frac{|A \cap B|}{|A| + |B| - |A \cap B|}$.

The limitation of the basic EsPRESSo protocol is that its performance depends on the total number of 3-grams that appear in the compared documents. To this end, the authors of [1] introduce an optimization based on the MinHash technique. In particular, instead of incorporating every available 3-gram in the corresponding 3-gram sets (A and B), Alice and Bob agree on k distinct hash functions ($H_1, H_2, \ldots, H_k$) to produce sets of size k, independent of the total number of 3-grams. Specifically, for $i \in \{1, 2, \ldots, k\}$, each party hashes all their 3-grams with the H_i hash function and select the digest with the minimum value as a representative in their respective set. Once sets A and B are constructed, the EsPRESSo protocol is invoked to compute the Jaccard index between the two documents. The MinHash approximation reduces considerably the computational and communication costs and is currently the state-of-the-art protocol in secure similar document detection.

3   Problem Definition

Bob (the server) holds a collection of N documents $\mathbb{D} = \{D_1, D_2, \ldots, D_N\}$. Each document $D_i \in \mathbb{D}$ is represented as a set of pairs $\langle w_i, f_i \rangle$, where w_i is a term appearing in the document and f_i is its frequency (i.e., the number of times it appears in the document). Alice (the client) holds a single document q that is represented in a similar fashion. Alice wants to know which documents in Bob's collection $\mathbb{D}$ are similar to q. Note that, if Alice herself holds a collection of M documents, the query is simply evaluated M distinct times.

In this work we propose two protocols with different privacy guarantees. The security of the basic protocol (Simhash, Sect. 4) is identical to the security provided by all existing SSDD protocols:

- For all $i \in \{1, 2, \ldots, N\}$, Alice learns the similarity score between q and D_i.
- Bob learns nothing.

On the other hand, the enhanced version of our protocol (Simhash*, Sect. 5) provides some additional security to the server (Bob):

- For all $i \in \{1, 2, \ldots, N\}$, Alice learns whether D_i's similarity score is above a user-defined threshold t (boolean value). The exact score remains secret.
- Bob learns nothing.

We assume that both parties could behave in an adversarial manner. Their goal is to derive any additional information other than the existence of similar documents and their similarity scores. For example, they could be interested in the contents of the other party's documents, statistical information about the terms in the other party's document collection, etc. Finally, we assume that both parties run in polynomial time and are "semi-honest," i.e., they will follow the protocol correctly, but will try to gain any advantage by analyzing the information exchanged during the protocol execution.

4   Basic Protocol

In this section we introduce our basic protocol that reveals the exact similarity score for each one of Bob's documents to Alice. Section 4.1 presents the protocol and Sect. 4.2 outlines its security proof.

4.1   The Simhash Protocol

Prior to protocol execution, each party runs a preprocessing step to generate the simhash fingerprints of their documents. The preprocessing includes lower case conversion, stop word removal, and stemming. In the end, each document is reduced to a set of terms and their corresponding frequencies. The simhash fingerprints are then created according to the algorithm described in Sect. 2.2. In what follows, we use a to denote Alice's simhash (from document q) and b_i ($i \in \{1, 2, \ldots, N\}$) to denote the simhash of document D_i in Bob's database. Recall that all fingerprints are binary vectors of size $l = 64$ bits.

Similarity based on simhash fingerprints is defined as the number of *non-matching* bits between the two bit vectors. In other words, a similarity score of 0 indicates two possibly identical documents, while larger scores characterize less similar documents. Consequently, it suffices to securely compute (i) the bitwise XOR of the two vectors and (ii) the summation of all bits in the resulting XOR

Simhash

Input: Alice has a simhash fingerprint a
            Bob has N simhash fingerprints $\{b_1, b_2, \ldots, b_N\}$
Output: Alice gets N similarity scores $\{\sigma_1, \sigma_2, \ldots, \sigma_N\}$

  Alice
1: Alice sends to Bob $E(a[0]), E(a[1]), \ldots, E(a[l-1])$;

  Bob
2: **for** $(i = 1; i \leq N; i++)$ **do**
3:    Set $\sigma_i \leftarrow 0$ and compute $E(\sigma_i)$;
4:    **for** $(j = 0; j < l; j++)$ **do**
5:      **if** $(b_i[j] == 0)$ **then**
6:        $E(\sigma_i) \leftarrow E(\sigma_i)E(a[j])$;
7:      **else**
8:        $E(\sigma_i) \leftarrow E(\sigma_i)E(1)E(a[j])^{-1}$;
9:      **end if**
10:   **end for**
11: **end for**
12: Bob sends to Alice $E(\sigma_1), E(\sigma_2), \ldots, E(\sigma_N)$;

  Alice
13: Alice decrypts all ciphertexts and retrieves $\sigma_1, \sigma_2, \ldots, \sigma_N$;

Fig. 2. The Simhash protocol

vector. Figure 2 shows the detailed protocol, where $E(\cdot)$ denotes encryption with Alice's ElGamal public key (which is known to Bob).

First (line 1), Alice encrypts every bit of her fingerprint a and sends l ciphertexts to Bob. Bob cannot decrypt these ciphertexts but is still able to blindly perform the required XOR and addition operations. In particular, for every document D_i in his database, Bob initializes the encryption of the similarity score to $E(\sigma_i) = E(0)$ (line 3). Next, he iterates over the l bits of the corresponding fingerprint b_i. If the bit at a certain position j is 0, then the result of the XOR operation is equal to $a[j]$ and Bob simply adds the value to the encrypted score (line 6). Otherwise, the result of the XOR operation is $(1 - a[j])$ which is also added to $E(\sigma_i)$ in a similar fashion (line 8). After all documents are processed, Bob sends the encrypted results to Alice (line 12). Finally, Alice uses her private key to decrypt the scores and identify the most similar documents to q (line 13).

4.2   Security

In this section we prove the security of the Simhash protocol for semi-honest adversaries, following the simulation paradigm [9]. In particular, we will show that, for each party, we can simulate the distribution of the messages that the party receives, given only the party's input and output in this protocol.

This is a sufficient requirement for security because, if we can simulate each party's view from only their respective input and output, then the messages themselves cannot reveal any additional information.

Alice's input consists of a bit vector a and her output is $\{\sigma_1, \sigma_2, \ldots, \sigma_N\}$. The only messages that Alice receives from Bob are the encryptions of the N similarity scores. The simulator knows Alice's public key and it also knows her output. Therefore, it can simply generate the encryptions of the corresponding scores.

In Bob's case, the input is N bit vectors and there is no output. In the beginning of the protocol, Bob receives l encryptions from Alice. Here, the simulator can simply generate l encryptions of zero. Given the assumption that the underlying encryption scheme is semantically secure, Bob cannot distinguish these ciphertexts from the ones that are produced by Alice's real input.

5 Enhanced Protocol

The basic Simhash protocol has the same security definition as all existing SSDD protocols in the literature. That is, Alice learns the similarity score for every document D_i in Bob's database. Nevertheless, making all this information available to Alice may allow her to construct some "malicious" queries that reveal whether a certain term (or 3-gram) exists in Bob's database. Consider the EsPRESSo protocol as an example. Alice's query may consist of a number of fake 3-grams (i.e., 3-grams that could not appear in Bob's documents) plus a real one that Alice wants to test against Bob's database. After completing the protocol execution, Alice can infer that the 3-gram is present in Bob's database if at least one of the similarity scores is non-zero. This attack is not as trivial to perform with the simhash or MinHash techniques, but it is still possible for sophisticated adversaries to devise similar attacks.

To this end, in this section, we introduce Simhash*, an enhanced version of the basic Simhash protocol that maintains the similarity scores secret. This is the first SSDD protocol in the literature that provides this functionality. In particular, Alice and Bob agree on a similarity threshold t and the protocol returns, for each document D_i, a boolean value θ_i that indicates whether $\sigma_i \leq t$. The detailed protocol is shown in Fig. 3.

The first steps of the protocol (lines 1–10) are identical to Simhash, i.e., Bob blindly computes the encryptions of all N similarity scores. However, instead of sending these ciphertexts to Alice, Bob computes, for each $D_i \in \mathbb{D}$, the encryptions of $r_j \cdot (\sigma_i - j)$ where $j \in \{0, 1, \ldots, t\}$ (lines 12–13). Specifically, r_j is a uniformly random value that masks the actual similarity score (σ_i) when it is not equal to j. On the other hand, if σ_i is equal to j, then the computed value is an encryption of 0. Next, Bob uses a random permutation π_i for each set of $(t+1)$ ciphertexts corresponding to document D_i, and eventually sends a total of $(t+1) \cdot N$ ciphertexts back to Alice (line 16). The different permutations are required in order to prevent Alice from inferring the value of j (i.e., similarity score) that produces the encryption of 0. Finally, Alice concludes that document

---

Simhash*

Input: Alice has a simhash fingerprint a
            Bob has N simhash fingerprints $\{b_1, b_2, \ldots, b_N\}$
Output: Alice gets N binary values $\{\theta_1, \theta_2, \ldots, \theta_N\}$

    Alice
1: Alice sends to Bob $E(a[0]), E(a[1]), \ldots, E(a[l-1])$;

    Bob
2: **for** $(i = 1; i \leq N; i{+}{+})$ **do**
3:     Set $\sigma_i \leftarrow 0$ and compute $E(\sigma_i)$;
4:     **for** $(j = 0; j < l; j{+}{+})$ **do**
5:       **if** $(b_i[j] == 0)$ **then**
6:         $E(\sigma_i) \leftarrow E(\sigma_i)E(a[j])$;
7:       **else**
8:         $E(\sigma_i) \leftarrow E(\sigma_i)E(1)E(a[j])^{-1}$;
9:       **end if**
10:    **end for**
11:    **for** $(j = 0; j \leq t; j{+}{+})$ **do**
12:      Choose r_j, uniformly at random from $\mathbb{Z}_p^*$;
13:      $E(x_{ij}) \leftarrow [E(\sigma_i)E(j)^{-1}]^{r_j}$;
14:    **end for**
15: **end for**
16: Bob sends to Alice $\{E(x_{ij})\}, \forall i \in \{1, 2, \ldots, N\}, j \in \pi_i(\{0, 1, \ldots, t\})$;

    Alice
17: Alice decrypts all ciphertexts and retrieves $\{x_{ij}\}$;
18: **for** $(i = 1; i \leq N; i{+}{+})$ **do**
19:    **for** $(j = 0; j \leq t; j{+}{+})$ **do**
20:      **if** $(x_{ij} == 0)$ **then**
21:        break;
22:      **end if**
23:    **end for**
24:    **if** $(j > t)$ **then**
25:      $\theta_i \leftarrow$ false;
26:    **else**
27:      $\theta_i \leftarrow$ true;
28:    **end if**
29: **end for**

Fig. 3. The Simhash* protocol

D_i's similarity score is within the predetermined threshold t, if and only if one of the $(t + 1)$ ciphertexts corresponding to D_i decrypts to 0 (lines 19–28).

    The security proof of the Simhash* protocol is trivial and follows the proof outlined in Sect. 4.2. In particular, only Alice's case is different, since (i) her output is N boolean values $\{\theta_1, \theta_2, \ldots, \theta_N\}$ and (ii) she receives $(t + 1) \cdot N$

ciphertexts from Bob. Nevertheless, the simulator knows Alice's output and also knows how the protocol operates. Therefore, for all documents D_i where θ_i is *true*, the simulator generates t random encryptions plus one encryption of 0. On the other hand, for documents where θ_i is *false*, the simulator generates $(t+1)$ random encryptions.

6 Experimental Evaluation

In this section we experimentally compare the performance of our methods against existing SSDD protocols. Section 6.1 describes the experimental setup and Sect. 6.2 illustrates the results of our experiments.

6.1 Setup

We compare our protocols against the work of Murugesan et al. [12] that utilizes cosine similarity (labeled as "Cosine" in our results), and EsPRESSo (both the basic protocol and the MinHash optimization) [1] that is based on 3-grams. We implemented all protocols in C++ and leveraged the GMP[2] library for handling large numbers. To ensure a fair comparison, we set the bit length of p (the order of the cyclic group G[3] in Fig. 1) to 160 bits, and the bit length of the RSA modulus in Paillier's cryptosystem to 1024 bits. This results in similar security levels for the underlying cryptographic protocols. We ran both the client and the server applications on a 2.4 GHz Intel Core i5 CPU. The performance metrics that we tested include the CPU time, the communication cost, and the precision/recall of the document retrieval process.

The document corpus is a collection of Wikipedia[4] articles. In particular, we selected 103 main articles from diverse topics and, for each article, we also selected a number (around 10) of its previous versions from the history pages of this topic. The total number of documents in the corpus is 1152. For Simhash and Cosine, we applied lower case conversion, stop word removal, and stemming, in order to derive the document terms along with their frequencies. For the EsPRESSo protocols, we extracted the 3-grams as explained in [1]. The total number of terms in the documents is 152,571 and the total number of 3-grams is 10,392.

6.2 Results

In the first set of experiments we investigate the document retrieval performance of the various protocols. The objective is to compare the underlying document representation methods: term vectors, simhash, and 3-grams. The experiments were performed as follows. We run 103 queries, where the query documents were

---

[2] http://gmplib.org
[3] Note that the EsPRESSo protocols are also implemented on top of group G.
[4] http://en.wikipedia.org

selected to be the most recent versions of the 103 unique articles. Using different threshold values, we observed the precision and soundness of the retrieved documents (recall that we know in advance the "correct" results, since the different versions of each article are very similar to each other). For our methods we used the threshold values $\{2, 3, 4, 5, 6\}$, while for the rest of the protocols we used the values $\{0.6, 0.7, 0.8, 0.9, 0.99\}$. Observe that, for Simhash, larger threshold values imply less similar documents, whereas for the other methods the opposite is true.

We used the *precision* and *recall* as the performance metrics for the document retrieval process. Precision is defined as:

$$precision = \frac{|R \cap V|}{|R|}$$

where R is the set of retrieved documents and V is the total number of documents that satisfy the query. In other words, precision is equal to the fraction of retrieved documents that belong to the result set. Recall, on the other hand, indicates the fraction of the result set that is retrieved by the query and is computed as:

$$recall = \frac{|R \cap V|}{|V|}$$

Figure 4(a) and (b) show the precision and recall curves for the various EsPRESSo protocols. As expected, the basic protocol has the best overall performance and maintains a precision of 1.0 for all threshold values. The MinHash approximations sacrifice some precision for better running times, but they all perform very well for threshold values larger than 0.7. In terms of recall, all EsPRESSo variants are very sensitive to the underlying threshold value, experiencing a large drop when the threshold is larger than 0.8. The Cosine method has a very stable performance, as shown in Fig. 4(c). In particular, both the precision and recall values remain over 0.75 under all settings. Finally, Simhash exhibits excellent query precision for all threshold values (Fig. 4(d)). Furthermore, the query recall raises steadily with increasing threshold values and, when the threshold is 6, Simhash retrieves over 96 % of the relevant documents.

In the next experiment we measure the computational cost of the various methods. We select MinHash-50 (i.e., MinHash with $k = 50$ hash functions) to represent the EsPRESSo family of protocols, since it has the best performance in terms of CPU time. The experiments were performed as follows. We run the cryptographic protocols for the 103 unique queries and measured the total CPU time, excluding the initial query encryption time (which is performed only once, independent of the database size N). From this value we determined the average time needed to compare a pair of documents. Using this measurement, Fig. 5 depicts the CPU time required to compare one document against a database of size N, where $N \in \{100, 500, 1000, 3000, 5000\}$ (the curves also include the query encryption time). Simhash is by far the best protocol among all competitors and it is one order of magnitude faster than MinHash-50. Cosine incurs a very high computational cost, mainly due to the query encryption step that involves tens

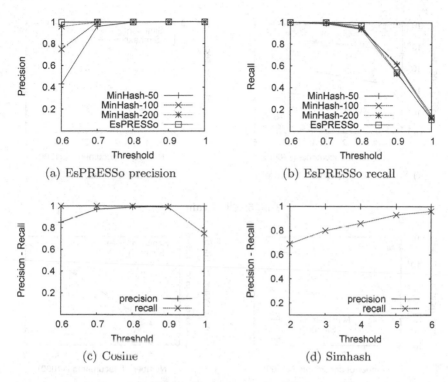

(a) EsPRESSo precision

(b) EsPRESSo recall

(c) Cosine

(d) Simhash

Fig. 4. Precision and recall

of thousands of public key encryptions. MinHash-50 is significantly slower than Simhash, because it involves numerous (expensive) modular exponentiations for every document in the server's database.

Figure 5(b) shows the CPU overhead of the Simhash* protocol, where the similarity threshold is set to $t = 6$. The additional cost is due to the $(t + 1)$ modular exponentiations that are required to hide a document's similarity score. However, Simhash* is considerably faster than MinHash-50, incurring 23.7 s of CPU time to compare 5000 documents, as opposed to 107.5 s for MinHash-50.

Figure 6(a) illustrates the communication cost for Simhash, MinHash-50, and Cosine. Clearly, Simhash outperforms significantly both competitor methods, incurring a communication cost that is at least 18 times smaller under all settings. For example, to compare one document against a database of size $N = 5000$, requires 1.24 MB of data communication for Simhash, 35.29 MB for MinHash-50, and 38.47 MB for Cosine. The drawback of MinHash-50 is that it has to send 50 ciphertexts plus 50 SHA-1 hashes for every document in the database. On the other hand, the overhead for Cosine lies exclusively on the transmission of the encrypted term vector, which is why it seems to remain unaffected by the database size N.

Finally, Fig. 6(b) shows the communication overhead for the Simhash* protocol. In this experiment, the threshold t is set to 6, which necessitates the

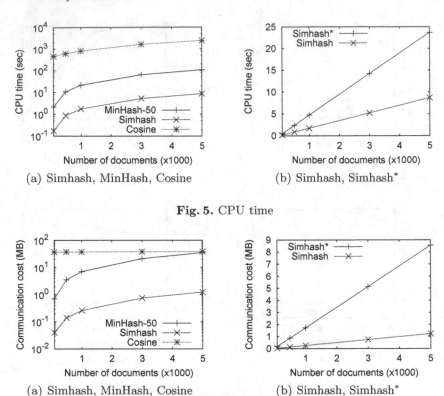

(a) Simhash, MinHash, Cosine   (b) Simhash, Simhash*

Fig. 5. CPU time

(a) Simhash, MinHash, Cosine   (b) Simhash, Simhash*

Fig. 6. Communication cost

transmission of 7 ciphertexts for every document in the database. As a result, the communication cost of Simhash* is around 7 times larger than the cost of the basic Simhash protocol. Nevertheless, it is still significantly lower than the competitor methods, requiring just 8.56 MB of data for $N = 5000$ documents.

7   Conclusions

Secure similar document detection (SSDD) is a new and important research area with numerous application domains, such as patent protection, intelligence collaboration, etc. In these scenarios, two parties want to identify similar documents within their databases, while maintaining their contents secret. Nevertheless, existing SSDD protocols are very expensive in terms of both computational and communication cost, which limits their scalability with respect to the number of documents. To this end, we introduce a novel solution based on simhash document fingerprints that is both simple and robust. In addition, we propose an enhanced version of our protocol that, unlike existing work, hides the similarity scores of the compared documents from the client. Through rigorous experimentation, we show that our methods improve the computational and communication costs by at least one order of magnitude compared to the current state-of-the-art protocol. Furthermore, they perform very well in terms of query precision and recall.

Acknowledgments. This research has been funded by the NSF CAREER Award IIS-0845262.

References

1. Blundo, C., De Cristofaro, E., Gasti, P.: EsPRESSo: efficient privacy-preserving evaluation of sample set similarity. In: Di Pietro, R., Herranz, J., Damiani, E., State, R. (eds.) DPM 2012 and SETOP 2012. LNCS, vol. 7731, pp. 89–103. Springer, Heidelberg (2013)
2. Charikar, M.: Similarity estimation techniques from rounding algorithms. In: STOC, pp. 380–388 (2002)
3. Cramer, R., Gennaro, R., Schoenmakers, B.: A secure and optimally efficient multi-authority election scheme. Eur. Trans. Telecommun. 8(5), 481–490 (1997)
4. Cristofaro, E.D., Gasti, P., Tsudik, G.: Fast and private computation of set inter-section cardinality. IACR Cryptology ePrint Archive 2011, 141 (2011)
5. ElGamal, T.: A public-key cryptosystem and a signature scheme based on discrete logarithms. IEEE Trans. Inf. Theory 31(4), 469–472 (1985)
6. Huang, L., Wang, L., Li, X.: Achieving both high precision and high recall in near-duplicate detection. In: CIKM, pp. 63–72 (2008)
7. Jiang, W., Murugesan, M., Clifton, C., Si, L.: Similar document detection with limited information disclosure. In: ICDE, pp. 735–743 (2008)
8. Jiang, W., Samanthula, B.K.: N-gram based secure similar document detection. In: Li, Y. (ed.) DBSec. LNCS, vol. 6818, pp. 239–246. Springer, Heidelberg (2011)
9. Lindell, Y., Pinkas, B.: Secure multiparty computation for privacy-preserving data mining. J. Priv. Confidentiality 1(1), 59–98 (2009)
10. Manber, U.: Finding similar files in a large file system. In: USENIX Winter, pp. 1–10 (1994)
11. Manku, G.S., Jain, A., Sarma, A.D.: Detecting near-duplicates for web crawling. In: WWW, pp. 141–150 (2007)
12. Murugesan, M., Jiang, W., Clifton, C., Si, L., Vaidya, J.: Efficient privacy-preserving similar document detection. VLDB J. 19(4), 457–475 (2010)
13. Naor, M., Pinkas, B.: Computationally secure oblivious transfer. J. Cryptology 18(1), 1–35 (2005)
14. Yao, A.C.C.: How to generate and exchange secrets. In: FOCS, pp. 162–167 (1986)

Big Security for Big Data: Addressing Security Challenges for the Big Data Infrastructure

Yuri Demchenko[1(✉)], Canh Ngo[1], Cees de Laat[1], Peter Membrey[2], and Daniil Gordijenko[3]

[1] University of Amsterdam, Amsterdam, The Netherlands
{y.demchenko,c.t.ngo,C.T.A.M.deLaat}@uva.nl
[2] Hong Kong Polytechnic University, Hong Kong, China
cspmembrey@comp.polyu.edu.hk
[3] Inoitech S.a.r.l., Luxembourg, Luxembourg
dgordijenko@inoitech.eu

Abstract. Big Data technologies are changing the traditional technology domains and their successful use will require new security models and new security design approaches to address emerging security challenges. This paper intends to provide initial analysis of the security issues and challenges in Big Data and map new challenges and problems to the traditional security domains and technologies. The paper starts with the Big Data definition and discusses the features that impact the most the Big Data security, such as Veracity, Volume, Variety, and dynamicity. The paper analyses the paradigm change and new challenges to Big Data security. The paper refers to the generic Scientific Data Infrastructure (SDI) model and discusses security services related to the proposed Federated Access and Delivery Infrastructure (FADI) that serves as an integration layer for potentially multi-provider multi-domain federated project oriented services infrastructure. The paper provides suggestions for practical implementation of such important security infrastructure components as federated access control and identity management, fine-grained data-centric access control policies, and the Dynamic Infrastructure Trust Bootstrap Protocol (DITBP) that allows deploying trusted remote virtualised data processing environment. The paper refers to the past and ongoing project experience by authors and discusses how this experience can be consolidated to address new Big Data security challenges identified in this paper.

Keywords: Big Data security · Federated Access and Delivery Infrastructure (FADI) · Trusted virtualised environment · Cloud infrastructure services

1 Introduction

Big Data and Data Intensive technologies are becoming a new technology trend in science, industry and business [1–3]. Big Data are becoming related to almost all aspects of human activity from just recording events to research, design, production and digital services or products delivery, to the final consumer. Current technologies such as Cloud Computing and ubiquitous network connectivity provide a platform for automation of all processes in data collection, storing, processing and visualization. Consequently, emerging data intensive technologies impose new challenges to

W. Jonker and M. Petković (Eds.): SDM 2013, LNCS 8425, pp. 76–94, 2014.
DOI: 10.1007/978-3-319-06811-4_13, © Springer International Publishing Switzerland 2014

traditional security technologies that may require re-thinking and re-factoring currently used security models and tools.

In e-Science and industry, the scientific data and technological data are complex multifaceted objects with the complex internal relations and typically distributed between different systems and locations. They are becoming an infrastructure of their own and need to be supported by corresponding physical or logical infrastructures to store, access, process and manage these data. We refer to such infrastructure as Scientific Data Infrastructure (SDI) or Big Data Infrastructure (BDI) in general. We argue that both SDI and BDI should provide capabilities to support collaborative groups of researchers or technologists due to complex character of the research projects or production processes.

The goal of this paper is to understand the main features, trends and new possibilities in Big Data technologies development, identify the security issues and problems related to the specific Big Data properties, and based on this to review existing security models and tools and evaluate their potentiality to be used with Big Data technologies.

There is no well-established terminology in the area of Big Data. Expectedly this problem will be solved by the recently established NIST Big Data Working Group [4]. In this paper we primarily focus on the security issues related to Big Data and in many case use terms Big Data technologies, Data Intensive Technologies and Big Data Science as interchangeable depending on the context.

The authors made an initial attempt in their recent papers [5, 6] to summarise related Big Data discussions and provide a definition of the 5V of Big Data: Volume, Velocity, Variety, Value, and Veracity, as the main properties of the Big Data that create a challenge to modern technologies. In this paper we continue with the Big Data definition and primarily focus on the security related aspects.

The paper is organised as follows. Section 2 looks into Big Data definition and Big Data nature in science, industry, and business, analyses factors that impact security. Section 3 gives a short overview of related research and developments. Section IV discusses security challenges to Big Data infrastructure and Big Data challenges to traditional security models. Section 4 discusses paradigm shift in Big Data security and new challenges to be addressed. Section 5 briefly discussed data management and proposes the Scientific Data Lifecycle Management model, identifies security and trust related issues in handling data, and summarises the general requirements and design suggestions for cloud based Big Data security infrastructure. Section 6 discusses the main components of the consistent cloud based security infrastructure for Big Data: Federated Access and Delivery Infrastructure, fine granular data centric policy definition, and Virtual Infrastructure Trust Bootstrapping protocol. Section 7 provides suggestions for the future research and developments.

2 Big Data Definition and Security Properties

2.1 Big Data Nature in e-Science, Industry and Business

We observe that Big Data "revolution" is happening in different human activity domains empowered by significant growth of the computer power, ubiquitous availability of computing and storage resources, increase of digital content production. To show the specifics of Big Data properties and use, we can distinguish the following Big Data domains: e-Science/research, industry, and business, leaving analysis of other domains for future research.

Science has been traditionally dealing with challenges to handle large volume of data in complex scientific research experiments, involving also wide cooperation among distributed groups of individual scientists and research organizations. Scientific research typically includes collection of data in passive observation or active experiments which aim to verify one or another scientific hypothesis. Scientific research and discovery methods are typically based on the initial hypothesis and a model which can be refined based on the collected data. The refined model may lead to a new more advanced and precise experiment and/or the previous data re-evaluation. The future SDI/BDI needs to support all data handling operations and processes providing also access to data and to facilities to collaborating researchers. Besides traditional access control and data security issues, security services need to ensure secure and trusted environment for researcher to conduct their research.

Big Data in industry are related to controlling complex technological processes and objects or facilities. Modern computer-aided manufacturing produces huge amount of data which are in general need to be stored or retained to allow effective quality control or diagnostics in case of failure or crash. Similarly to e-Science, in many industrial applications/scenarios there is a need for collaboration or interaction of many workers and technologists.

In business, private companies will not typically share data or expertise. When dealing with data, companies will intend always to keep control over their information assets. They may use shared third party facilities, like clouds or specialists instruments, but special measures need to be taken to ensure workspace safety and data protection, including input/output data sanitization.

With the digital technologies proliferation into all aspects of business activities, the industry and business are entering a new playground where they need to use scientific methods to benefit from the new opportunities to collect and mine data for desirable information, such as market prediction, customer behavior predictions, social groups activity predictions, etc. Refer to numerous blog articles [3, 7, 8] suggesting that the Big Data technologies need to adopt scientific discovery methods that include iterative model improvement and collection of improved data, re-use of collected data with improved model.

2.2   5 Vs of Big Data and Data Veracity

Despite the "Big Data" became a new buzz-word, there is no consistent definition for Big Data, nor detailed analysis of this new emerging technology. Most discussions are going now in blogosphere where active contributors have generally converged on the most important features and incentives of the Big Data [2, 8–10]. In our recent paper [6] we summarised existing definitions and proposed a consolidated view on the generic Big Data features that was used to define the general requirements to Scientific

Data Infrastructure. In this paper we provide a short summary and discuss the main Big Data properties that impose new security challenges.

For the completeness of the discussion, we quote here the IDC definition of Big Data (rather strict and conservative): "A new generation of technologies and architectures designed to economically extract value from very large volumes of a wide variety of data by enabling high-velocity capture, discovery, and/or analysis" [10]. It can be complemented more simple definition from [11]: "Big Data: a massive volume of both structured and unstructured data that is so large that it's difficult to process using traditional database and software techniques." This is also in accordance with the definition given by Jim Gray in his seminal book [12].

We refer to the Big Data definition proposed in our recent paper [6] as having the following 5V properties: Volume, Velocity, Variety, Value, and Veracity, as illustrated in Fig. 1. We also highlight the security related properties Veracity, Variety and Volume (by the density of the property representing circles).

(1) Veracity

Veracity property of Big Data is directly related to the Big Data security and includes two aspects: data consistency (or certainty) what can be defined by their statistical reliability; and data trustworthiness that is defined by a number of factors including data origin, collection and processing methods, including trusted infrastructure and facility.

Big Data veracity ensures that the data used are trusted, authentic and protected from unauthorised access and modification. The data must be secured during the whole their lifecycle from collection from trusted sources to processing on trusted compute facilities and storage on protected and trusted storage facilities.

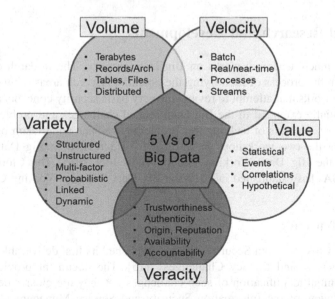

Fig. 1. 5 Vs of Big Data and security related properties of Veracity, Variety, and Volume.

The following aspects define and need to be addressed to ensure data veracity:

- Integrity of data and linked data (e.g., for complex hierarchical data, distributed data with linked metadata)
- Data authenticity and (trusted) origin.
- Identification of both data and source.
- Computer and storage platform trustworthiness.
- Availability and timeliness.
- Accountability and Reputation.

Data veracity relies entirely on the security infrastructure deployed and available from the Big Data infrastructure. Data provenance is an important mechanism to ensure data Veracity.

(2)   Other impact factors: Volume, Variety and Dynamicity

Security and privacy issues are magnified by volume, variety, and Big Data dynamicity (or variability). The latter is originated from the fact that data change their structure, model, content, and may migrate between datacenters and clouds during their lifecycle.

Volume as the main generic feature of the Big Data provides also challenges to current security technologies that need to scale the size of Big Data, also taking into account their distributed character.

Dynamicity and data linkage are the two other factors that reflect changing or evolving character of data and need to keep their linkage during the whole their lifecycle. This will require scalable provenance models and tools incorporating also data integrity and confidentiality.

3   Related Research and Developments

There is not much academic works on Big Data security. The research community currently is in the process of identifying the potential research areas. However, many new research works that attempt to review the very basic security concepts and models can be potentially extended to the Big Data related challenges and problems.

First serious attempts of tackling this problem have been undertaken by the NIST by organising the two workshops in 2012 and 2013 related to Big Data [13] and establishing the Big Data Working Group [4] in July 2013. The Cloud Security Alliance (CSA) has established in 2012 the Big Data Security Working Group [14].

3.1   CSA Top Ten

Recently the CSA Big Data Security WG has published its first deliverable "Top Ten Big Data Security and Privacy Challenges" [15]. The document provides a good insight and initial identification of such challenges but they are clearly defined from the point of view of the Information Security and Service Management and don't touch security design issues. In our research and in this paper, we approach the Big

Data Security problem from the Security Engineering point of view, providing also analysis of existing security technologies and their applicability and required modification to support Big Data infrastructure and processes.

We find useful to provide a short summary of the CSA Top Ten (refer to the original document [15] for details). We group them into few clusters:

A. Infrastructure security
   (1) Secure computations in distributed programming frameworks.
   (2) Security best practices for non-relational data stores.
   (3) Secure data storage and transactions logs.
   (4) End-point input validation/filtering.

B. Access control and policy
   (5) Granular access control and data centric access policies.
   (6) Cryptographically enforced access control and secure communication.

C. Data Management
   (7) Real-time security/compliance monitoring.
   (8) Granular audits.
   (9) Data provenance.

D. Privacy and Confidentiality
   (10) Scalable and composable privacy-preserving data mining and analytics.

In this paper, we will discuss different aspects of securing Big Data, identify new security challenges and propose generic security mechanisms to address these challenges.

3.2 Related Security Research

Most of currently used security models, services and mechanisms have been developed for host based, client/server, or service oriented models. Big Data have their specific security requirements, new business models and actors with different relations, and also global scalability character. All this will motivate changing current security services and development of new models and services. For the related research, besides specifically dealing with the Big Data security, we can look also at the recent research that attempt to respond to the changing landscape of the services and technologies with emerging global computing environment, ubiquitous connectivity and proliferation of personal devices, and growth of data centric applications, in particular in healthcare, behavioral and bio-science.

We found a number of interesting conceptual and innovative papers presented at the New Security Paradigms Workshop in the past 3 years. In particular, paper [16] looks at a new "clean slate" approach to the security problems originated from the healthcare that currently becomes increasingly computerized and data intensive. The healthcare use case can be one of reference cases to solve the whole bunch of the data protection related problems. Paper [17] analyses the VM and services virtualization based security models and evaluate their effectiveness. Paper [18] looks at the privacy as a process and attempts to provide a theoretical basis for new/future Privacy Enhancing Technologies (PET).

We can also refer to the related work presented at the SDM12 workshop. Paper [19] proposes an approach to build a trustworthy cloud platform motivated by the specific requirements from the healthcare applications to the trustworthiness of the healthcare platforms. The proposed solution is based on using federated cloud-of-cloud architecture to enforce common security and data protection policies in various cloud layers. Paper [20] discusses new provenance models for complex multi-source Web 2.0 data that similar to Big Data can evolve with time.

We find appropriate also to refer to our past works that attempted to review and re-factor different key security problems related to Grid security [21] and cloud security [22].

4   Paradigm Shift and New Challenges

4.1   Paradigm Shift to Data Centric Security

Traditional security models are OS/system based and host/service centric what means the security is either communication protocols based or ensured by the system/OS based security services. The security and administrative domains are the key concepts, around which the security services and protocols are built. A domain provides a context for establishing security context and trust relation. This creates a number of problems when data (payload or session context) are moved from one system to another or between domains.

Big Data will require different data centric security protocols, especially in the situation that the object or event related data will go through a number of transformations and become even more distributed, between traditional security domains. The same relates to the current federated access control model that is based on the cross administrative and security domains identities and policy management. Keeping security context and semantic integrity, to support data provenance in particular, will require additional research.

The following are additional factors that will create new challenges and motivate security paradigms change in Big Data security:

- Virtualization: can improve security of data processing environment but cannot solve data security "in rest".
- Mobility of the different components of the typical data infrastructure: sensors or data source, data consumer, and data themselves (original data and staged/evolutional data). This in its own cause the following problems.

  - On-demand infrastructure services provisioning.
  - Inter-domain context communication.

- Big Data aggregation that may involve data from different administrative/logical domains and evolutionally changing data structures (also semantically different).
- Policy granularity: Big Data may have complex structure and require different and high-granular policies for their access control and handling.

4.2 Trusted Virtualisation Platforms

In many cases the companies or users need to store or process their data on the provider facilities in the environment that is not under their control. In most cases they can rely on the provider's business practices but in some cases, both commercially and privacy sensitive, this is not sufficient. Virtualisation technologies enhanced with the trusted computing technologies can potentially provide a basis for developing proper solutions here.

Traditional secure virtualization models are domain and host based. Advancements in services virtualisation (e.g. using Java service container [23]) and developments of the wide scale cloud virtualization platforms [24] provide a sufficiently secure environment for runtime processes but still rely on the trusted hardware and virtualization/hypervisor platform. To address key data-centric (and ownership based) security model it needs to be empowered with the Trusted Computing Platform security mechanisms, in particular, implementing the remote platform trust bootstrapping protocol. We discuss such possible solution in Sect. 6.

4.3 Data Ownership

Data ownership will become one of the important concepts in data management and policy definition. Data ownership concept is widely discussed in the context of data governance and personal data protection [25], but there is no well-defined mechanisms to enforce data ownership related policies in the distributed data processing environment. Data centric ownership model is a cross-domain and needs to span the whole data lifecycle. In this respect it is different from the current facility ownership concept in IT, telecommunications and clouds, which is rather provider and domain based. Data ownership is linked to individual or organisational ownership and will affect many currently used security concepts such as identity centric access control and delegation (like implemented in the Auth2.0 protocol [26]), user centric federation and trust model, identity based trust model and data protection mechanisms, data verifiability/audibility.

Federated security models need to adopt the data ownership concept and allow building data centric cross-domains federations. It is also understood that data ownership will impact data provenance and lifecycle management model.

4.4 Personal Information, Privacy and Opacity

Modern services and infrastructure supporting social networks and human activity are tending to be of the scale of humanity, i.e. scaling world-wide (like Facebook) or targeting to support the knowledge base of the whole humanity (like Wikipedia). Their notion of Big Data actually means "ALL (relevant) data". Such systems are unavoidably dealing with the personal identifiable information, despite using existing techniques for information de-identification and anonymisation.

Lot of information can be collected about individuals and privacy protection concerns are known in this area. Big Data will motivate developments of the new privacy protection models in this area. Acknowledging general requirement to protect privacy and personal data, we still think that existing privacy concepts and PET models will change with the Big Data technologies development and proliferation.

Healthcare system, governmental systems, defense and law enforcement systems will increasingly collect more and more information about individuals. In many cases such information is vitally important for health, life and security. On the other hand, business and service industry will also increasingly collect more information than it is needed to conduct their main business. With modern analytics tool, additional not intended personal information can be extracted from such datasets/collections by linking different datasets and/or applying behavioral analysis.

There is another aspect of the confidentiality or privacy when providing shared datasets services which we define as opacity. The researchers who are in many cases doing competitive research on the shared datasets and/or facilities,like in case of the genome research or LHC experiment, need to trust that their activity (in particular data accessed or applications used) is not tracked and cannot be seen by other competitors. The computing facilities need to make the individual activity opaque although retaining the possibility for data provenance and audit.

5 Security Infrastructure for Big Data

5.1 Scientific Data Lifecycle Management (SDLM)

In Big Data, security needs to be provided consistently during the whole data lifecycle. The generic data lifecycle includes at least the following stages: data acquisition/collection; filtering and classification; processing and analytics; visualization and delivery.

The scientific data lifecycle is more complex and includes a number of consequent stages: research project or experiment planning; data collection; data processing; publishing research results; discussion, feedback; archiving (or discarding).

The required new approach to data management and handling in e-Science is reflected in the proposed by the authors the Scientific Data Lifecycle Management (SDLM) model [6, 27], (see Fig. 2). The SDLM incorporates both the existing practices researched in [28] and current trends in the Data Intensive Science.

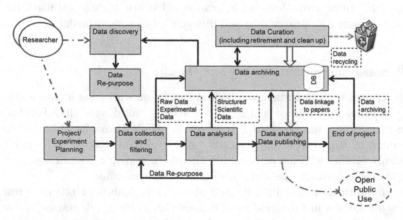

Fig. 2. Scientific Data Lifecycle Management in e-Science

The new SDLM requires data storage and preservation at all stages what should allow data re-use/re-purposing and secondary research on the processed data and published results. However, this is possible only if the full data identification, cross-reference and linkage are implemented in SDI.

Capturing information about the processes involved in transformation from raw data up until the generation of published data becomes an important aspect of scientific data management. Scientific data provenance becomes an issue that also needs to be taken into consideration by SDI providers [29].

Another factor that will define the SDLM and SDI requirements is the European Commission's initiative to support Open Access [30] to scientific data from publicly funded projects suggests introduction of the following mechanisms to allow linking publications and data: persistent data ID (PDI) [31], and Open Researcher and Contributor Identifier (ORCID) [32].

Data integrity, access control and accountability must be supported during the whole data during lifecycle. Data curation is an important component of the discussed SDLM and must also be done in a secure and trustworthy way.

5.2 Security and Trust in Cloud Based Infrastructure

Ensuring data veracity in Big Data infrastructure and applications requires deeper analysis of all factors affecting data security and trustworthiness during their whole lifecycle. Figure 3 illustrates the main actors and their relations when processing data on remote system. User/customer and service provider are the two actors concerned with their own data/content security and each other system/platform trustworthiness: users want to be sure that their data are secure when processed or stored on the remote system.

Figure 3 illustrates the complexity of trust and security relations even in a simple usecase of the direct user/provider interaction. In clouds data security and trust model needs to be extended to distributed, multi-domain and multi-provider environment.

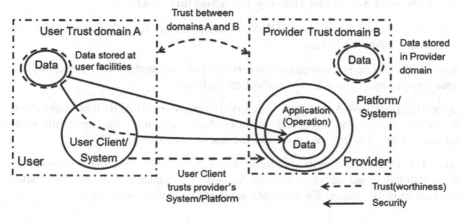

Fig. 3. Security and Trust in Data Services and Infrastructure.

5.3   General Requirements to Security Infrastructure

To support secure data processing, the future SDI/BDI should be supported by an corresponding security infrastructure that would ensure normal infrastructure operation, assets and information protection, and allow user identification/authentication and policy enforcement in distributed multi-organisational environment.

Moving to Open Access [30] may require partial change of business practices of currently existing scientific information repositories and libraries, and consequently the future Access Control and Accounting Infrastructure (ACAI) should allow such transition and fine grained access control and flexible policy definition and control.

Taking into account that future SDI/BDI should support the whole data lifecycle and explore the benefit of the data storage/preservation, aggregation and provenance in a large scale and during long/unlimited period of time, the future ACAI should also support all stages of the data lifecycle, including policy attachment to data to ensure persistency of the data policy enforcement during continuous online and offline processes [33].

The required ACAI should support the following features:

- Empower researchers (and make them trust) to do their data processing on shared facilities of large datacentres with guaranteed data and information security.
- Motivate/ensure researchers to share/open their research environment to other researchers by providing tools for instantiation of customised pre-configured infrastructures to allow other researchers to work with existing or own data sets.
- Protect data policy, ownership, linkage (with other data sets and newly produced scientific/research data), when providing (long term) data archiving. (Data preservation technologies should themselves ensure data readability and accessibility with the changing technologies).

6   SDI/BDI Security Infrastructure Components

6.1   Federated Access and Delivery Infrastructure (FADI)

In [6] we proposed the generic SDI Architecture model for e-Science (e-SDI) that contains the following layers:

Layer D6: User side and campus based services that may include user portals, identity management services and also visualization facilities.

Layer D5: Federated Access and Delivery Infrastructure (FADI) that interconnects Federation and Policy layer that includes federation infrastructure components, including policy and collaborative user groups support functionality.

Layer D4: (Shared) Scientific platforms and instruments (including potentially distributed/global sensor network) specific for different research areas that also include high performance clusters for Big Data analytics and shared datasets.

Layer D3: Infrastructure virtualisation layer that is represented by the Cloud/Grid infrastructure services and middleware supporting specialised scientific platforms deployment and operation.

Layer D2: Datacenters and computing resources/facilities.

Layer D1: Network infrastructure layer represented by the general purpose Internet infrastructure and dedicated network infrastructure.

Note: "D" prefix denotes relation to data infrastructure.

The proposed SDI reflects the main components required to process, consume and manage data and can easily adopted to the general Big Data Infrastructure.

Modern cloud technologies provide a proper basis for implementing SDI/BDI, in particular for Layer D3 and Layer D4 that correspondingly provide the general infrastructure virtualization platform and shared scientific platform and instruments that typically provide services on-demand for dynamically created virtual groups of users, also called Virtual Organisations. The main efforts to create and operate infrastructure for specific scientific projects will be put into the Layer D5 Federated Access and Delivery Infrastructure (FADI).

When implemented in clouds, the FADI and SDI in general may involve multiple providers and both cloud and non-cloud based infrastructure components. Our vision and intention is to use for this purpose the general Intercloud Architecture Framework (ICAF) proposed in our works [34]. ICAF provides a common basis for building adaptive and on-demand provisioned multi-provider cloud based services.

Figure 4 illustrates the general architecture and the main components of the FADI (that corresponds to the ICAF Access and Delivery Layer C5) that includes infrastructure components to support inter-cloud federations services such as Cloud Service Brokers, Trust Brokers, and Federated Identity Provider. Each service/cloud

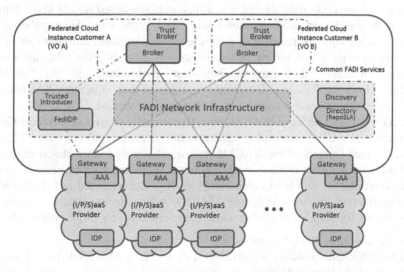

Fig. 4. Federated Access and Delivery Infrastructure (FADI)

domain contains an Identity Provider IDP, Authentication, Authorisation, Accounting (AAA) service and service gateway that typically communicates with other domains.

FADI incorporates related federated infrastructure management and access technologies [34–36]. Using federation model for integrating multi-provider heterogeneous services and resources reflects current practice in building and managing complex infrastructures (SDI and enterprise infrastructures) and allows for inerorganisational resource sharing.

6.2   Data Centric Access Control

SDI/BDI will incorporate standards and if needed advance access control services and mechanisms at the level of FADI and users/services level. However consistent data centric security and access control will require solving the following problems:

- Fine-granular access control policies.
- Encryption enforced attribute based access control.

Depending on the data type and format, the two basic access control and policy models can be defined: resource and/or document based access control, including intra document; and cell or record based access control for data stored in databases. We identify XACML policy language as appropriate for document/intra-document access control. For databases we need to combine their native access control mechanisms and general document based access control.

(1) XACML policies for fine granular access control
The policies for data centric access control model should provide the fine-grained authorization features, based not only on the request context attributes such as subjects/users, data identifiers, actions or lifetimes, but also on the structured data content. A prospective direction is to design and apply attribute based access control mechanisms with policies incorporate along with data granularity. Such policies may contain complex logic expressions of attributes. Based on input attribute values from users, their queries could return either authorized data or errors. In this respect, managing SDI/BDI big data using attribute-based policy languages like XACML is applicable. However, for large documents or complex data structures XACML policies evaluation may create a significant performance overhead.

We refer to our experience in developing Dynamically provisioned Access Control Infrastructure (DACI) for complex infrastructure services and resources [22, 37]. It uses advanced features of the XACML based policies that allow describing access control rules for complex multi-domain resources, including domain, session context, multi-domain identity and trust delegation [38–40]. The proposed in [41] the Multi-data-types Interval Decision Diagrams (MIDD) policy decision request evaluation method allows for significant performance gain for massively large policy sets.

(2) Access control in NoSQL databases
The popular NoSQL databases for structured data storage MongoDB [42], Cassandra [43], Accumulo [44] provide different levels of security and access control. Most of them have coarse-grain authorization features, both on user management and on

protected data granularity like table-level or row-level security. Accumulo [44] provides the most advanced features to allow cell-level security with which accesses from keys to values are only granted when the submitted attributes satisfy predefined Boolean expressions provided as a security label of the cell key index. However, the current policy language in Accumulo is at early development stage and lacks of features for distributed, multi-domains environments.

(3) Encryption enforced access control
Described above solutions are capable to address majority of the problems for data access, transfer and processing stages, however data in-rest when stored on remote facilities may remain unprotected. The solution to this problem can be found with using the encryption enhanced access control policies that in addition to the traditional access control, use also attributes based encryption [45, 46] to allow data decryption only to the targeted subject or attribute owner. We admit such approach as potentially effective and applicable to many data protection use cases in Big Data, in particular, healthcare or targeted broadcast of streaming data that make take place when using distributed sensor networks.

6.3   Trusted Infrastructure Bootstrapping Protocol

To address the issues with creating trusted remote/distributed environment for processing sensitive data, in our earlier papers [47, 48] we proposed a generic Dynamic Infrastructure Trust Bootstrapping Protocol (DITBP). This includes supporting mechanisms and infrastructure that takes advantage of the TCG Reference Architecture (TCGRA) and Trusted Platform Module (TPM) [49, 50]. The TPM is used to provide a root of trust that extends from the physical hardware itself, and to generate a key pair in hardware where the private key is never revealed (i.e. non-migratable).

There are four functional components to support the bootstrapping process:

Domain Authentication Server (DAS) provides a trusted root for the third party's domain.

Bootstrap Initiator (BI) is the application that is transferred to the remote machine in order to confirm the machine's status before any infrastructure or software is deployed.

Bootstrap Requester (BREQ) is a client application that runs on the machine responsible for provisioning remote infrastructure. It communicates with its counterpart on the remote machine and handles the first/initial stage of the bootstrapping process.

Bootstrap Responder (BRES) is the counterpart server application. It is responsible for authenticating the machine to a remote client and verifying that the client is authorized to bootstrap the machine. Once each end point has been authenticated, the BRES will receive, decrypt and decompress the payload sent by the client.

The bootstrapping process includes the following 4 steps:

(1)   Initially the BRES on the target machine, registers and authenticates itself with the DAS. This done over a TCP connection. Hardware based keys from the TPM are used to authenticate the instance and complete the handshake. Key data is then signed and stored on the DAS.
(2)   When the BREQ needs to authenticate a target machine, it connects to the DAS and authenticates itself. This authentication could be simple user and password based authentication, or could also involve security tokens or pre-shared certificates and keys.
(3)   After authentication, the DAS provides the BREQ with the certificates and keys for the target machine. The BREQ then constructs a bootstrapping request with an encrypted payload containing the Bootstrap Initiator (BI), secured using the provided credentials. This requests is then sent to the DAS over the same authenticated TCP channel. The DAS then signs and forwards the request with the encrypted payload to the BRES.
(4)   As the payload is encrypted with the target machines public key / certificate which is tied to the TPM (non-migratable keypair), only the target machine is able to decrypt the payload. Once decrypted, the BRES executes the BI and hands control over to it. The BI can effectively execute any code on the machine and thus can verify that the machine and the platform are as expected and as required. Once complete, the BI can then download the infrastructure payload (this would be implementation specific) and can then execute it and hand over control to the framework.

A prototype implementation of the BREQ and BRES is called Yin and Yang and described in [48]. The NodeJS and SocketIO libraries, provide a two-way message framework that allows the focus to remain on the message content and their structure. NodeJS has bindings for NaCl which provide a range of cryptographic functions. At present there is no native binding for TPM functionality, however initially software generated keys and certificates can be exchanged for developing and verifying the protocol.

7   Future Research and Development

The authors will continue their research to understand the new challenges and required solutions for Big Data infrastructure and applications. The future research and development will include further enhancement of the Big Data definition. This should provide a better basis for proposing a consistent Big Data security model and architecture addressing identified security challenges presented in this paper. At this stage we tried to review existing security technologies, own experience and consolidate them around the main security problems in Big Data such as providing trusted virtualized environment for data processing and storing, fine granular access control, and general infrastructure security for scientific and general Big Data applications.

The authors will also continue working on the data centric and user centric security models that should also incorporate new Big Data properties such as data ownership. A number of technical security problems will arise with the implementation of persistent data and researcher identifiers (PID and ORCID), as required by the new EC initiative, and related privacy and provenance issues.

As a part of the general infrastructure research we will continue research on the infrastructure issues in Big Data targeting more detailed and technology oriented definition of SDI and related security infrastructure definition. Special attention will be given to defining the whole cycle of the provisioning SDI services on-demand, specifically tailored to support instant scientific workflows using cloud IaaS and PaaS platforms. This research will be also supported by development of the corresponding Cloud and InterCloud architecture framework to support the Big Data e-Science processes and infrastructure operation.

The authors will look also at the possibility to contribute to the standardisation activity at the Research Data Alliance (RDA) [51] and recently established NIST Big Data Working Group [4].

References

1. Global Research Data Infrastructures: Towards a 10-year vision for global research data infrastructures. Final Roadmap, March 2012. http://www.grdi2020.eu/Repository/FileScaricati/6bdc07fb-b21d-4b90-81d4-d909fdb96b87.pdf
2. Reflections on Big Data, Data Science and Related Subjects: Blog by Irving Wladawsky-Berger. http://blog.irvingwb.com/blog/2013/01/reflections-on-big-data-data-science-and-related-subjects.html
3. Roundup of Big Data Pundits' Predictions for 2013. Blog post by David Pittman. 18 Jan 2013. http://www.ibmbigdatahub.com/blog/roundup-big-data-pundits-predictions-2013
4. NIST Big Data Working Group (NBD-WG). http://bigdatawg.nist.gov/home.php/
5. Demchenko, Y., Zhao, Z., Grosso, P., Wibisono, A., de Laat, C.: Addressing big data challenges for scientific data infrastructure. In: The 4th IEEE Conference on Cloud Computing Technologies and Science (CloudCom2012), Taipei, 3–6 Dec 2012
6. Demchenko, Y., Membrey, P., Grosso, P., de Laat, C.: Addressing big data issues in scientific data infrastructure. In: First International Symposium on Big Data and Data Analytics in Collaboration (BDDAC 2013). Proceeding. The 2013 International Conference on Collaboration Technologies and Systems (CTS 2013), San Diego, 20–24 May 2013
7. The Forrester Wave: Big Data Predictive Analytics Solutions: Q1 2013. Mike Gualtieri, 31 Jan 2013. http://www.forrester.com/pimages/rws/reprints/document/85601/oid/1-LTEQDI
8. Dumbill, E.: What is big data? An introduction to the big data landscape. http://strata.oreilly.com/2012/01/what-is-big-data.html
9. The 3Vs that define Big Data. Posted by Diya Soubra on 5 July 2012. http://www.datasciencecentral.com/forum/topics/the-3vs-that-define-big-data
10. IDG IDC's Latest Digital Data Study: A Deep Dive, Blogpost by Mary Ludloff. http://blog.patternbuilders.com/2011/07/08/idcs-latest-digital-data-study-deep-dive/
11. The Big Data Long Tail. Blog post by Jason Bloomberg on 17 Jan 2013. http://www.devx.com/blog/the-big-data-long-tail.html

12. The Fourth Paradigm: Data-Intensive Scientific Discovery. Hey, T., Tansley, S., Tolle, K. (eds.) Microsoft Corporation, Oct 2009. ISBN: 978-0-9825442-0-4. http://research. microsoft.com/en-us/collaboration/fourthparadigm/
13. NIST Big Data Workshop, 13–14 June 2012. http://www.nist.gov/itl/ssd/is/big-data.cfm
14. CSA Big Data Working Group. https://cloudsecurityalliance.org/research/big-data/
15. Expanded Top Ten Big Data Security and Privacy Challenges. CSA Report, 16 June 2013. https://downloads.cloudsecurityalliance.org/initiatives/bdwg/Expanded_Top_Ten_Big_Data _Security_and_Privacy_Challenges.pdf
16. Peisert, S., Talbot, E., Bishop, M.: Turtles all the way down: a clean-slate, ground-up, first-principles approach to secure systems. In: Proceedings of the 2012 Workshop on New Security Paradigms, NSPW '12. ACM, New York (2012)
17. Bratus, S., Locasto, M., Ramaswamy, A., Smith, S.: VM-based security overkill: a lament for applied systems security research. In: Proceedings of the 2010 Workshop on New Security Paradigms, NSPW '10. ACM, New York (2010)
18. Morton, A., Sasse, A.: Privacy is a process, not a pet: a theory for effective privacy practice. In: Proceeding NSPW '12 Proceedings of the 2012 Workshop on New Security Paradigms. ACM, New York (2012). ISBN: 978-1-4503-1794-8
19. Deng, M., Nalin, M., Petković, M., Baroni, I., Marco, A.: Towards trustworthy health platform cloud. In: Jonker, W., Petković, M. (eds.) SDM 2012. LNCS, vol. 7482, pp. 162–175. Springer, Heidelberg (2012)
20. Bienvenu, M., Deutch, D., Suchanek, F.M.: Provenance for Web 2.0 data. In: Jonker, W., Petković, M. (eds.) SDM 2012. LNCS, vol. 7482, pp. 148–155. Springer, Heidelberg (2012)
21. Demchenko, Y., de Laat, C., Koeroo, O., Groep, D.: Re-thinking grid security architecture. In: Proceedings of IEEE 4th Science 2008 Conference, pp. 79–86. IEEE Computer Society Publishing, Indianapolis, 7–12 Dec 2008. ISBN: 978-0-7695-3535-7
22. Demchenko, Y., Ngo, C., de Laat, C., Wlodarczyk, T., Rong, C., Ziegler, W.: Security infrastructure for on-demand provisioned cloud infrastructure services. In: Proceedings of 3rd IEEE Conference on Cloud Computing Technologies and Science (CloudCom2011), 29 Nov–1 Dec 2011, Athens, Greece, ISBN: 978-0-7695-4622-3
23. Oracle Fusion Middleware Security Guide: Overview Java Security Models. http://docs. oracle.com/cd/E12839_01/core.1111/e10043/introjps.htm
24. Hypervisors, virtualization, and the cloud: learn about hypervisors, system virtualization, and how it works in a cloud environment. By Bhanu P. Tholeti, IBM. http://www.ibm.com/ developerworks/cloud/library/cl-hypervisorcompare/
25. Prins, C.: When personal data, behavior and virtual identities become a commodity: would a property rights approach matter? J. Law Technol. Soc. 3(4) (2006). http://www2.law.ed. ac.uk/ahrc/script-ed/vol3-4/prins.pdf (SCRIPT-ed)
26. RFC6749: The OAuth 2.0 authorization framework. http://tools.ietf.org/html/rfc6749
27. European Union: A study on authentication and authorisation platforms for scientific resources in Europe. European Commission, Brussels 2012. Final Report. Contributing author. Internal identification SMART-Nr 2011/0056. http://cordis.europa.eu/fp7/ict/ e-infrastructure/docs/aaa-study-final-report.pdf
28. Data Lifecycle Models and Concepts. http://wgiss.ceos.org/dsig/whitepapers/ Data%20Lifecycle%20Models%20and%20Concepts%20v8.docx
29. Koopa, D., et al.: A provenance-based infrastructure to support the life cycle of executable papers. In: International Conference on Computational Science, ICCS 2011. http://vgc. poly.edu/~juliana/pub/vistrails-executable-paper.pdf
30. Open access: opportunities and challenges. European Commission for UNESCO. http://ec. europa.eu/research/science-society/document_library/pdf_06/open-access-handbook_en.pdf

31. OpenAIR – Open access infrastructure for research in Europe. http://www.openaire.eu/
32. Open Researcher and Contributor ID. http://about.orcid.org/
33. Demchenko, Y., Lopez, D.R., Garcia Espin, J.A., de Laat, C.: Security services lifecycle management in on-demand infrastructure services provisioning. International Workshop on Cloud Privacy, Security, Risk and Trust (CPSRT 2010). In: 2nd IEEE International Conference on Cloud Computing Technology and Science (CloudCom2010), Indianapolis, 30 Nov–3 Dec 2010
34. Demchenko, Y., Makkes, M., Strijkers, R., Ngo, C., de Laat, C.: Intercloud architecture framework for heterogeneous multi-provider cloud based infrastructure services provisioning. Int. J. Next-Gener. Comput. (IJNGC) 4(2) (2013)
35. Makkes, M., Ngo, C., Demchenko, Y., Strijkers, R., Meijer, R., de Laat, C.: Defining intercloud federation framework for multi-provider cloud services integration. In: The 4th International Conference on Cloud Computing, GRIDs, and Virtualization (CLOUD COMPUTING 2013), Valencia, Spain, 27 May–1 June 2013
36. eduGAIN - Federated access to network services and applications. http://www.edugain.org
37. Ngo, C., Membrey, P., Demchenko, Y., De Laat, C.: Policy and context management in dynamically provisioned access control service for virtualized cloud infrastructures. In: 2012 7th International Conference on Availability, Reliability and Security (ARES), pp. 343–349, 20–24 Aug 2012
38. Ngo, C., Demchenko, Y., de Laat, C.: Toward a dynamic trust establishment approach for multi-provider intercloud environment. In: Proceedings of 2012 IEEE 4th International Conference on Cloud Computing Technology and Science (CloudCom), pp. 532–538, 3–6 Dec 2012
39. Demchenko, Y., Gommans, L., de Laat, C.: Using SAML and XACML for complex resource provisioning in grid based applications. In: Proceedings of IEEE Workshop on Policies for Distributed Systems and Networks (POLICY 2007), Bologna, Italy, 13–15 June 2007
40. Demchenko, Y., Cristea, M., de Laat, C.: XACML Policy profile for multidomain Network Resource Provisioning and supporting authorisation infrastructure. In: IEEE International Symposium on Policies for Distributed Systems and Networks (POLICY 2009), London, UK, 20–22 July 2009
41. Ngo, C., Makkes, M., Demchenko, Y., de Laat, C.: Multi-data-types interval decision diagrams for XACML evaluation engine. In: 11th International Conference on Privacy, Security and Trust 2013 (PST 2013), 10–12 July 2013 (to be published)
42. MongoDB. http://www.mongodb.org/
43. Apache Cassandra. http://cassandra.apache.org/
44. Apache Accumulo. http://accumulo.apache.org/
45. Goyal, V., Pandeyy, O., Sahaiz, A., Waters, B.: Attribute-based encryption for fine-grained access control of encrypted data. In: Proceedings of the 13th ACM Conference on Computer and Communications Security, CCS '06. http://research.microsoft.com/en-us/um/people/vipul/abe.pdf
46. Chase, M.: Multi-authority attribute based encryption. In: Vadhan, S.P. (ed.) TCC 2007. LNCS, vol. 4392, pp. 515–534. Springer, Heidelberg (2007). http://cs.brown.edu/~mchase/papers/multiabe.pdf
47. Demchenko, Y., Gommans, L., de Laat, C.: Extending user-controlled security domain with TPM/TCG in grid-based virtual collaborative environment. In: Proceedings The 2007 International Symposium on Collaborative Technologies and Systems (CTS 2007), pp. 57–65, Orlando, 21–25 May 2007. ISBN: 0-9785699-1-1

48. Membrey, P., Chan, K.C.C., Ngo, C., Demchenko, Y., de Laat, C.: Trusted virtual infrastructure bootstrapping for on demand services. In: The 7th International Conference on Availability, Reliability and Security (AReS 2012), Prague, 20–24 Aug 2012. ISBN: 978-0-7695-4775-6
49. Yahalom, R., Klein, B., Beth, T.: Trust relationships in secure systems-a distributed authentication perspective. In: Proceedings of the 1993 IEEE Computer Society Symposium on Research in Security and Privacy, pp. 150–164. IEEE (1993)
50. Brickell, E., Camenisch, J., Chen, L.: Direct anonymous attestation. In: Proceedings of the 11th ACM Conference on Trust and Security in Computer Systems (2004). http://portal. acm.org/citation.cfm?id=1030083.1030103
51. Research Data Alliance (RDA). http://rd-alliance.org/

Query Log Attack on Encrypted Databases

Tahmineh Sanamrad[(✉)] and Donald Kossmann

Department of Computer Science, Swiss Federal Institute of Technology,
Zurich, Switzerland
{Tahmineh.Sanamrad,Donald.Kossmann}@inf.ethz.ch

Abstract. Encrypting data at rest has been one of the most common
ways to protect the database data against honest but curious adversaries.
In the literature there are more than a dozen mechanisms proposed on
how to encrypt data to achieve different levels of confidentiality. However, a database system is more than just data. An inseparable aspect of
a database system is its interaction with the users through queries. Yet,
a query-enhanced adversary model that captures the security of user
interactions with the encrypted database is missing. In this paper, we
will first revisit a few well-known adversary models on the data encryption schemes. Also, to model the query-enhanced adversaries we additionally need new tools, which will be formally defined. Eventually, this
paper introduces query-enhanced adversary models which additionally
have access to the query logs or interact with the database in different
ways. We will prove by reduction that breaking a cryptosystem by a
query-enhanced adversary is at least as difficult as breaking the cryptosystem by a common adversary.

Keywords: Database encryption · Query Rewrite Function · Query-
enhanced adversary models

1   Introduction

In the recent past, there has been significant interest in processing queries on
encrypted data without decrypting the data. The goal is to protect the confidentiality of data against honest but curious attackers who have powerful access
rights on the machines that host and process the data; e.g., system administrators with root privileges. There has been a lot of work on proposing query-able
data encryption schemes such as [1,4–7,11].

However, data is not the only source of information for the adversary in a
database system. Interactions with a database through queries and transactions
might also lead to confidentiality leaks. Thus, in order to prove the level of
data confidentiality in a database system, it does not suffice to only look at the
adversary models which solely operate on the data. Therefore, new and enhanced
adversary models are required to capture the confidentiality of the database
query logs. The goal in this paper is to introduce such enhanced adversary models
that independent of the encryption scheme try to break the cryptosystem by

W. Jonker and M. Petković (Eds.): SDM 2013, LNCS 8425, pp. 95–107, 2014.
DOI: 10.1007/978-3-319-06811-4_14, © Springer International Publishing Switzerland 2014

looking at the query logs. So far there has been no single work dedicated to model the query log attack on encrypted databases.

In this paper we assume to have a client-server architecture, where the client is trusted and the database server is completely untrusted. We assume to have a thin encryption layer residing on a trusted party, either on the client itself or on a trusted security middleware. This thin encryption layer sits between the client and the untrusted database server. The main task of the encryption layer is to adjust the plaintext queries written by the clients in such a way that the encrypted database can process them. Upon receiving the query results, the encryption layer decrypts the result sets and sends them back to the client. Client is assumed to be unaware of the encryption layer in between, i.e. the encryption layer is transparent to the client. This model is assumed by almost all the database systems supporting encryption such as [2,6,8,10,12,14].

Now the main problem is how secure are these rewritten queries that are submitted to the untrusted database server. The encryption layer rewrites the queries based on the encryption scheme used to encrypt the data. There are however a number of examples on how the queries may leak additional information to the adversary. For example, some queries can reveal secrets about their underlying encryption scheme. Additionally, the query log itself provides the adversary with additional information about the client submitting the query, timestamp and submission frequency.

Since in a database system, data and queries are intertwined we need to carefully separate these two during security analysis. In the beginning of this paper we will explain the assumed architecture in more detail. Then, we will revisit the well-known adversary models on encrypted data, namely Ciphertext-only Attack, Known-Plaintext Attack and Chosen-Plaintext Attack. More concretely, this paper makes the following contributions:

- First contribution of this paper is the introduction and formal definition of new tools required to analyze a query-enhanced adversary, such as a one-way Query Rewrite Function (QRF) that takes an encryption scheme and an original query from the client as input and outputs a rewritten query for the encrypted database, a Query Simulator (QSim) that can simulate rewritten queries just by looking at the query logs and the encrypted data, and a Query Generator (QGen) that can generate original queries out of plaintext values.
- Second contribution of this paper are the query-enhanced adversary models.
- Third contribution is to prove that regardless of the chosen encryption scheme, the security guarantee that a database encryption scheme can give against a query-enhanced adversary is at least as much as the security guarantee that the database encryption scheme can give against a common adversary.

This paper is structured as follows: Sect. 2 revisits the common attacker scenarios on encrypted data. Afterward, Sect. 3 introduces the formal notions that will serve as building blocks in the query-enhanced adversary models. Eventually, Sect. 4 introduces the query-enhanced adversary models and proves by reduction that analyzing the security of the query logs can be replaced by the common security analysis on the underlying encryption scheme.

2   Preliminaries

In this section, we will first go over our assumptions regarding the system's architecture and security. Then, we revisit a few well-known attacks on the encryption schemes, namely Ciphertext-only Attack, Known-Plaintext Attack and Chosen-Plaintext Attack.

2.1   Client-Server Architecture

Figure 1a shows the traditional client-server architecture of running applications on top of a database system. The application or end user issues SQL statements to the database server. The database server executes these SQL statements and returns the results.

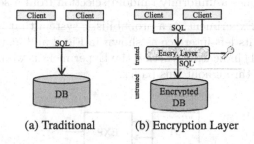

(a) Traditional   (b) Encryption Layer

Fig. 1. Extended Client-server Database Architecture

Figure 1b shows an abstraction of the security-extended architecture. In this architecture, the application is unchanged and issues the same (unencrypted) SQL statements as in the traditional system of Fig. 1a. In the following we will describe each component and its security assumptions in the security-extended architecture.

- **Encrypted DB** is the database server containing the encrypted data. In this paper the database server and all its components (e.g. main memory, CPU, ...) are assumed to be untrusted, however the server is not actively malicious.
- **Encryption Layer** implements the confidentiality. This layer can be seen as a trusted server namely a security middleware as in [6,10,13,14], it can be seen as a secure co-processor within the database server as in [2,3], or it can be an added module on the client's machine. The critical assumption is that this layer is trusted. The encryption layer is responsible for adjusting (rewriting) the queries to be processed on the encrypted data, and thereafter this layer needs to decrypt and if necessary post-process the query results.

– **Client** can be an end user or an application developer and is assumed to be trusted.

2.2 Attacks on Ciphers

In this section we go over the most common attack scenarios on the encryption schemes. These scenarios will be used in the reduction proofs in Sect. 4, where we define the query-enhanced adversaries.

Notation. Let x denote a plaintext value from the set of plaintext values, $\mathcal{X}$. Respectively, let y denote a ciphertext value from the set of ciphertext values, $\mathcal{Y}$. Let $\mathcal{E}nc(\tau, \mathbf{x})$ be the encryption function of an arbitrary encryption scheme, $\mathcal{ES}$ and τ the randomness element possibly required by the $\mathcal{E}nc$ function. $\mathbf{x} \xleftarrow{\$} \mathcal{X}$ simply means that a vector of plaintext elements have been chosen uniformly at random. The $\$$ implies a uniformly random selection from a set.

Experiment. An Experiment[1] is a probabilistic system that is connected to an Adversary[2], $\mathcal{A}$, on its left interface as shown in Fig. 2 and at the right interface outputs a bit (0 or 1) indicating whether the Experiment is won. The Experiment is denoted as EXP throughout this paper.

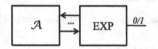

Fig. 2. An Experiment interacts with an adversary and in the end shows whether the adversary has succeeded.

Adversary. An adversary (attacker) is (or has access to) an algorithm that interacts with the experiment and its goal is to succeed in the experiment. The adversary is denoted as $\mathcal{A}$.

Advantage. The advantage of an adversary, $\mathcal{A}$, playing an experiment, EXP, is the success probability of $\mathcal{A}$ winning EXP, i.e. The experiment outputs 1 on its right interface. The advantage of $\mathcal{A}$ succeeding in EXP is denoted as $Adv^{\mathrm{EXP}}(\mathcal{A})$.

Ciphertext-only Attack (CoA). In a *Ciphertext-only Attack* the attacker is given only a series of ciphertexts for some plaintext unknown to the attacker [9]. If an attacker can succeed in a *Ciphertext-only Attack*, it means that he could succeed in the following experiment:

---

[1] An Experiment is also called a Game in some security literatures.
[2] An Adversary is also called a Winner in some security literatures.

Experiment 1 : $\mathrm{Exp}_{ES}^{CoA}(A)$

$\tau \xleftarrow{\$} \mathcal{T}; \mathbf{x} \xleftarrow{\$} \mathcal{X}$

$\mathbf{y} \leftarrow \mathcal{E}nc_{ES}(\tau, \mathbf{x})$

$x \xleftarrow{\$} A(\mathbf{y})$

if $x \in \mathbf{x}$ then return 1

else return 0

Experiment 1 chooses uniformly at random a vector of plaintext values, $\mathbf{x}$. It then encrypts them using the $\mathcal{E}nc_{ES}(\tau, \mathbf{x})$ function to obtain a vector of the corresponding ciphertext values, $\mathbf{y}$. The adversary then receives $\mathbf{y}$ and runs $A(\mathbf{y})$. The adversary succeeds if the plaintext value he returns, is in the plaintext vector chosen in the beginning by the experiment, in other words A succeeds if $x \in \mathbf{x}$. The advantage of the Ciphertext-only attacker on an arbitrary encryption scheme, $\mathcal{ES}$, is denoted as: $Adv_{ES}^{CoA}(A)$.

Known-Plaintext Attack (KPA). In a *Known-Plaintext Attack* the attacker is given a couple of plaintext-ciphertext pairs [9]. The goal of the attacker is to distinguish pairs of ciphertexts based on the plaintext they encrypt which were not initially given. Indistinguishability under *Known-Plaintext Attack* is captured through the following experiment:

Experiment 2 : $\mathrm{Exp}_{ES}^{IND\text{-}KPA}(A)$

$\tau \xleftarrow{\$} \mathcal{T}; \mathbf{x} \xleftarrow{\$} \mathcal{X}$

$\mathbf{y} \leftarrow \mathcal{E}nc_{ES}(\tau, \mathbf{x})$

$(x_1, x_2) \xleftarrow{\$} \mathcal{X}$ s.t. $x_1, x_2 \notin \mathbf{x}$

$b \xleftarrow{\$} \{0, 1\}$

$y_b \leftarrow \mathcal{E}nc_{ES}(\tau, x_b)$

$b' \xleftarrow{\$} A(\mathbf{x}, \mathbf{y}, (x_1, x_2), y_b)$

if $b' = b$ then return 1

else return 0

Experiment 2 chooses uniformly at random a vector of plaintext values, $\mathbf{x}$. It then encrypts these values using the $\mathcal{E}nc_{ES}(\tau, \mathbf{x})$ function to obtain a vector of the corresponding ciphertext values, $\mathbf{y}$. Then the experiment chooses randomly two plaintext values, (x_1, x_2) s.t. $x_1, x_2 \notin \mathbf{x}$, flips a coin and encrypts randomly one of them, $y_b = \mathcal{E}nc_{ES}(\tau, x_b)$. The attacker is then given both $\mathbf{x}$ and $\mathbf{y}$, (x_1, x_2) and y_b. Based on y_b and the information he may extract from the known Plaintext-Ciphertext pairs, $\mathbf{x}$ and $\mathbf{y}$, the attacker tries to find out whether x_1 or x_2 was encrypted. The probability that an attacker can succeed in this experiment is denoted as the IND-KPA advantage, $Adv_{ES}^{IND\text{-}KPA}(A)$ and is optimal if an attacker cannot do better than to randomly guess b, i.e. $Adv_{ES}^{IND\text{-}KPA}(A) \leq \frac{1}{2}$.

Chosen-Plaintext Attack (CPA). In a *Chosen-Plaintext Attack* the attacker is given plaintext-ciphertext pairs for the plaintext vector chosen by the attacker [9]. The goal of the attacker is to distinguish pairs of ciphertexts based on the plaintext they encrypt which were not initially chosen by the attacker. Therefore, the attacker, A, consists of two functions $A = (A_1, A_2)$. A_1 chooses a vector of plaintext values and A_2 tries to distinguish which plaintext was encrypted. Indistinguishability under *Chosen-Plaintext Attack* is captured through Experiment 3.

Experiment 3 : $\mathbf{Exp}_{\mathrm{ES}}^{\mathrm{IND\text{-}CPA}}(A)$

$\tau \xleftarrow{\$} \mathcal{T}; \ \mathbf{x} \leftarrow A_1(\mathcal{X})$

$\mathbf{y} \leftarrow \mathcal{E}nc_{\mathrm{ES}}(\tau, \mathbf{x})$

$(x_1, x_2) \leftarrow A_1(\mathcal{X}) \ s.t. \ x_1, x_2 \notin \mathbf{x}$

$b \xleftarrow{\$} \{0, 1\}$

$y_b \leftarrow \mathcal{E}nc_{\mathrm{ES}}(\tau, x_b)$

$b' \xleftarrow{\$} A(\mathbf{x}, \mathbf{y}, (x_1, x_2), y_b)$

if $b' = b$ **then return** 1

else return 0

The adversary, using A_1, chooses a vector of plaintext values, $\mathbf{x}$, and gives it to the experiment. The experiment encrypts these values using the $\mathcal{E}nc_{\mathrm{ES}}(\tau, \mathbf{x})$ function to obtain a vector of the corresponding ciphertext values, $\mathbf{y}$. Then, the adversary again chooses two plaintext values, $(x_1, x_2) \ s.t. \ x_1, x_2 \notin \mathbf{x}$ and gives it to the experiment. The experiment flips a coin and encrypts randomly one of them, $y_b = \mathcal{E}nc_{\mathrm{ES}}(\tau, x_b)$. The attacker is then given both $\mathbf{x}$ and $\mathbf{y}$, (x_1, x_2) and y_b. Based on y_b and the information he may extract from his chosen Plaintext-Ciphertext pairs, $\mathbf{x}$ and $\mathbf{y}$, the attacker tries to find out whether x_1 or x_2 was encrypted. The probability that an attacker can succeed in this experiment is denoted as the IND-CPA advantage, $Adv_{\mathrm{ES}}^{\mathrm{IND\text{-}CPA}}(A)$ and is optimal if an attacker cannot do better than to randomly guess b, i.e. $Adv_{\mathrm{ES}}^{\mathrm{IND\text{-}CPA}}(A) \leq \frac{1}{2}$.

3   New Definitions

In order to define new and query-enhanced adversary models we need additional functions that can capture the query transformations in the client-server architecture mentioned in Sect. 2.1.

Notation. Let the set of all queries a client sends to the encryption layer be denoted as $\mathcal{Q}_x$ and the set of rewritten-queries by the encryption layer to be processed on the encrypted database be $\mathcal{Q}_y$. Respectively, an original query submitted from the client is denoted as $q_x \in \mathcal{Q}_x$ and similarly a rewritten query submitted to the untrusted and encrypted database server is denoted as $q_y \in \mathcal{Q}_y$. $\mathcal{Q}_x^s$ denotes a subset of queries from $\mathcal{Q}_x$ and respectively, $\mathcal{Q}_y^s \subseteq \mathcal{Q}_y$.

Query. In this paper whenever we talk about a query, an SQL query is meant. However, our query-enhanced adversary models can be used also for other type of queries (e.g. information retrieval queries).

Running Example. Consider a relation $customer(id,name,age,salary,city)$ in the encrypted database. The following query, q_x, is sent by the client to the database server:

```
SELECT SUM(salary) FROM customer
    WHERE city = 'Zurich' and age <= 30
```

Since the database is encrypted, the client's query is intercepted by the encryption layer and rewrites the query in a way, so that it can be processed by the encrypted database.

Query Tokens. These tokens are the pieces of data in the SQL query. Query tokens can be in plaintext, for example given the query of our running example, the query tokens are 'Zurich' and 30. Query Tokens can also be in ciphertext.

Query Rewrite Function (QRF). The *Query Rewrite Function* is a function that takes an original query q_x, and an encryption scheme $\mathcal{ES}$ as input and outputs the rewritten query q_y, $QRF(\mathcal{ES}, q_x) = q_y$. Depending on the encryption scheme, q_x will be rewritten differently. For example, having data encrypted in the database with the deterministic AES, the query of our running example, q_x, is rewritten as follows $QRF(AES, q_x) = q_y$:

```
SELECT salary,age FROM customer
    WHERE city = EncAES('Zurich')
```

Why the rewritten query having a deterministic AES scheme looks like above is not in the scope of this paper. In brief, deterministic AES is neither homomorphic (no support for the SUM aggregate function), nor order preserving (no support for the range condition), but it is deterministic and therefore equality-preserving.

Query Generator (QGen). The *Query Generator* is a function that takes a vector of plaintext query tokens, $\mathbf{x}$, as input and generates a set of SQL queries Q_x^s using the tokens in $\mathbf{x}$. QGen is independent of the encryption scheme, $\mathcal{ES}$. QGen has an inverse function, $\mathbf{x} = QGen^{-1}(Q_x^s)$ which outputs the plaintext query tokens of its input set. Figure 3, shows how QGen works for our running example.

Query Simulator (QSim). Parallel to QGen but in the ciphertext space, the *Query Simulator* takes a vector of ciphertext query tokens, $\mathbf{y}$, as input and generates a set of SQL queries, Q_y^s, using the tokens in $\mathbf{y}$. QSim is independent of the encryption scheme and is allowed to use the query logs in Q_y. QSim has an inverse function too, $\mathbf{y} = QSim^{-1}(Q_y^s)$. Figure 4, shows how QSim works for our running example, assuming that $Enc_{AES}('Zurich') = EG42KL23$.

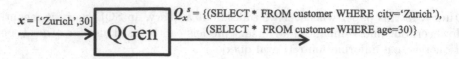

Fig. 3. QGen takes plaintext query tokens as input and builds a set of SQL queries out of them.

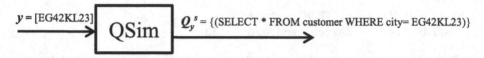

Fig. 4. QSim takes ciphertext query tokens as input and builds a set of rewritten SQL queries out of them.

Remark 1. *QGen and QSim are functions that do not change their input, x and y respectively, but wrap them in an SQL query.*

Figure 5, illustrates the above introduced functions. These functions will serve as building blocks in our adversary models and proofs.

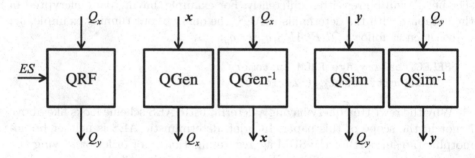

Fig. 5. Basic functions used in the query log adversary models

In the remainder of this section, we introduce and formally define the adversary models. We prove that each adversary model on the query logs can be reduced to a known adversary model on the underlying encryption scheme.

4   Adversary Models

Database Adversary: Let us define the database adversary, A^{DB}, to be an adversary that has access to everything on the database server, namely the set of rewritten queries, $\mathcal{Q}_y$, the encrypted data, $\mathcal{Y}$, and eventually the encrypted result sets which are the result of running $\mathcal{Q}_y$ on $\mathcal{Y}$. We also assume that the database schema is public, i.e. a database adversary knows about the tables, attributes, attribute types, foreign keys and so on.

Proof by Reduction: To prove that Problem B (with unknown complexity) is at least as hard as Problem A (with known complexity), one solves Problem A using the solver of Problem B. It suffices to find an efficient[3] transformation, ϕ between the Solver of Problem B, $\mathcal{T}$ into the Solver of Problem A, $\mathcal{S}$, i.e. $\mathcal{S} = \phi(\mathcal{T})$.

4.1   Query-Only Attack

Query-only Attack (abbreviated as QoA) is when the database adversary A^{DB} has only access to the rewritten query logs namely, $\mathcal{Q}_y$. The advantage of a database adversary, A^{DB}, to succeed in a *Query-only Attack*, is defined as his probability to win the Experiment 4:

$$Adv_{\mathrm{ES}}^{\mathrm{QoA}}(A^{\mathrm{DB}}) = Pr[Exp_{\mathrm{ES}}^{\mathrm{QoA}}(A^{\mathrm{DB}}) = 1]$$

The experiments $Exp_{\mathrm{ES}}^{\mathrm{QoA}}(A^{\mathrm{DB}})$ is defined as follows:

Experiment 4 : $\mathbf{Exp}_{\mathrm{ES}}^{\mathrm{QoA}}(A^{\mathrm{DB}})$

$\mathbf{x} \xleftarrow{\$} \mathcal{X}$
$Q_x^S \leftarrow QGen(\mathbf{x})$
$Q_y^S \leftarrow QRF(\mathcal{ES}, Q_x^S)$
$x_\iota \xleftarrow{\$} A^{\mathrm{DB}}(Q_y^S)$
if $x_\iota \subset \mathbf{x}$ **then return** 1
else return 0

In the following we will prove that the *Ciphertext-only Attack* discussed in detail in Sect. 2 can be reduced to a Query-only Attack.

Lemma 1. *Given an encryption scheme $\mathcal{ES}$ and a subset of rewritten queries, $Q_y^S \in \mathcal{Q}_y$, $\mathcal{ES}$ is at least as safe against Query-only Attack as $\mathcal{ES}$ is safe against Ciphertext-only Attack.*

$$Adv_{\mathrm{ES}}^{QoA}(A^{DB}) \leq Adv_{\mathrm{ES}}^{CoA}(A)$$

Proof. Let $\mathcal{ES}$ be an arbitrary encryption scheme. Suppose A^{DB} is an adversary with non-trivial QoA advantage against $\mathcal{ES}$. We construct a *Ciphertext-only* adversary A against $\mathcal{ES}$. As per definition in the Ciphertext-only Experiment 1, A is given a vector of encrypted values, $\mathbf{y}$. A runs $QSim(\mathbf{y})$ to simulate Q_y^S. Eventually, A runs $A^{\mathrm{DB}}(Q_y^S)$. A's communication with A^{DB} mimics the QoA experiment. Clearly, A is efficient since $QSim$ is sublinear to the size of its input.

---
[3] Polynomial-time in the size of the input.

4.2   Known-Query Attack

Known-Query Attack (abbreviated as KQA) is when the database adversary A^{DB} has access to a number of (q_x, q_y) pairs. For example assume q_x is:

```
SELECT SUM(salary) FROM customer
  WHERE city = 'Zurich' and age <= 30
```

then q_y using a deterministic $\mathcal{ES}$ will be something like:

```
SELECT salary, age FROM customer
  WHERE city = Enc_ES('Zurich')
```

Remark 2. *Query Logs additionally provide a database adversary with information about the clients submitting the queries, timestamp of the query submitted and their frequency. An adversary that has background knowledge about the business logic can use these additional log information to guess the original queries submitted by the clients. In general, statistical attacks on query logs can be classified as KQA.*

The advantage of a database adversary, A^{DB}, to succeed in a *Known-Query Attack*, is defined as his probability to distinguish the rewrite of two queries with the same structure as shown in the Experiment 5.

$$Adv_{ES}^{IND\text{-}KQA}(A^{DB}) = Pr[Exp_{ES}^{IND\text{-}KQA}(A^{DB}) = 1]$$

The experiments $Exp_{ES}^{IND\text{-}KQA}(A^{DB})$ is defined as follows:

Experiment 5 : $\mathbf{Exp_{ES}^{IND\text{-}KQA}}(A^{DB})$

$Q_x^S \xleftarrow{\$} Q_x$
$Q_y^S \leftarrow QRF(\mathcal{ES}, Q_x^S)$
$(q_x^1, q_x^2) \xleftarrow{\$} Q_x$ s.t. $q_x^1, q_x^2 \notin Q_x^S$
$b \xleftarrow{\$} \{0, 1\}$
$q_y^b \leftarrow QRF(\mathcal{ES}, q_x^b)$
$b' \xleftarrow{\$} A(Q_x^S, Q_y^S, (q_x^1, q_x^2), q_y^b)$
if $b' = b$ **then return** 1
  else return 0

Lemma 2. *Given an encryption scheme $\mathcal{ES}$ and a set of original and rewritten query pairs, (Q_x^S, Q_y^S), $\mathcal{ES}$ is at least as safe[4] against Known-Query Attack as $\mathcal{ES}$ is safe against Known-Plaintext Attack.*

$$Adv_{ES}^{IND\text{-}KQA}(A^{DB}) \leq Adv_{ES}^{IND\text{-}KPA}(A)$$

---

[4] Safe means indistinguishable in this experiment.

Proof. Let $\mathcal{ES}$ be an arbitrary encryption scheme. Suppose A^{DB} is an adversary with non-trivial *IND-KQA* advantage against $\mathcal{ES}$. We construct an *IND-KPA* adversary, A, against $\mathcal{ES}$. As per definition in the IND-KPA experiment (Experiment 2), A is given a set of plaintext-ciphertext pairs. A has also access to a limited QRF that only works for Q_x^S. A first runs $QGen(\mathbf{x}) = Q_x^S$ and then $QRF(\mathcal{ES}, Q_x^S) = Q_y^S$. Additionally, A receives x_1, x_2 and y_b, so he constructs $q_x^1 = QGen(x_1)$, $q_x^2 = QGen(x_2)$ and $q_y^b = QSim(y_b)$. Eventually, A runs $A^{DB}(Q_x^S, Q_y^S, (q_x^1, q_x^2), q_y^b)$. A's communication with A^{DB} mimics the IND-KQA experiment. Clearly, A is efficient since $QGen$, QRF and $QSim$ are linear to the size of their input.

Indistinguishability against *Known-Plaintext Attack* (Sect. 2) can be reduced to indistinguishability against *Known-Query Attack* as Lemma 2 shows.

4.3 Chosen-Query Attack

Chosen-Query Attack (abbreviated as CQA) is when the database adversary, A^{DB}, has access to a Query Rewrite Function, $QRF(\mathcal{ES})$. For example, an adversary that can send arbitrary queries to the encryption layer and see the rewritten queries on the other end. The advantage of a database adversary, $A^{CQA} = (A^{CQ}, A^{DB})$, to succeed in a *Chosen-Query Attack*, is defined as his probability to distinguish the rewrite of his chosen queries as shown in Experiment 6.

$$Adv_{ES}^{IND\text{-}CQA}(A^{CQA}) = Pr[Exp_{ES}^{IND\text{-}CQA}(A^{CQA}) = 1]$$

The indistinguishability against *Chosen-Plaintext Attack* (see Sect. 2) can be reduced to indistinguishability against *Chosen-Query Attack* as Lemma 3 suggests.

Experiment 6 : $\mathrm{Exp}_{ES}^{IND\text{-}CQA}(A^{CQA})$

$Q_x^S \xleftarrow{\$} A^{CQ}(Q_x)$
$Q_y^S \leftarrow QRF(\mathcal{ES}, Q_x^S)$
$(q_x^1, q_x^2) \leftarrow A^{CQ}(Q_x)$ s.t. $q_x^1, q_x^2 \notin Q_x^S$
$b \xleftarrow{\$} \{0,1\}$
$q_y^b \leftarrow QRF(\mathcal{ES}, q_x^b)$
$b' \xleftarrow{\$} A(Q_x^S, Q_y^S, (q_x^1, q_x^2), q_y^b)$
if $b' = b$ **then return** 1
else return 0

Lemma 3. *Given an encryption scheme $\mathcal{ES}$ and a set of original and rewritten query pairs, $(\mathcal{Q}_x^S, \mathcal{Q}_y^S)$ where Q_x^S has been chosen by the adversary, $\mathcal{ES}$ is at least as safe against a Chosen-Query Attack as $\mathcal{ES}$ is safe against a Chosen-Plaintext Attack.*

$$Adv_{ES}^{IND\text{-}CQA}(A^{CQA}) \leq Adv_{ES}^{IND\text{-}CPA}(A)$$

Proof. Let $\mathcal{ES}$ be an arbitrary encryption scheme. Suppose A^{CQA} is an adversary with non-trivial *IND-CQA* advantage against $\mathcal{ES}$. We construct a *CPA* adversary A against $\mathcal{ES}$. As per definition in the IND-CPA experiment (Experiment 3), A is given a set of plaintext-ciphertext pairs where plaintexts have been chosen by the attacker. A has also access to a full-fledged QRF. A first runs $QGen(\mathbf{x})$ $= Q_x^S$ and then $QRF(\mathcal{ES}, Q_x^S) = Q_y^S$. Additionally, A receives x_1, x_2 and y_b, so he constructs $q_x^1 = QGen(x_1)$, $q_x^2 = QGen(x_2)$ with the same structure and $q_y^b = QSim(y_b)$.

Eventually, A runs $A^{\mathrm{DB}}(Q_x^S, Q_y^S, (q_x^1, q_x^2), q_y^b)$. A's communication with A^{CQA} mimics the IND-CQA experiment. Clearly, A is efficient since $QGen$, QRF and $QSim$ are linear to the size of their input.

5   Conclusion

In this paper we have shown why it is important to consider additional and enhanced adversary models when analyzing the security of an encrypted database. The reason is because an encrypted database does not only consist of data but also queries and therefore, the security of the query logs are as important as the security of the data. Along the way, we have introduced a few notions and tools such as a Query Rewrite Function, a Query Generator and a Query Simulator to be used in our query-enhanced adversary models. In the end, we proved by reduction that breaking a database encryption using a query-enhanced adversary is at least as hard as breaking the underlying encryption scheme using a normal adversary. More concretely, we could show in this paper that:

- An encrypted database is at least as secure against a Query-only Attack as its underlying encryption scheme is secure against a Ciphertext-only Attack
- An encrypted database is at least as secure against a Known-Query Attack as its underlying encryption scheme is secure against a Known-Plaintext Attack
- An encrypted database is at least as secure against a Chosen-Query Attack as its underlying encryption scheme is secure against a Chosen-Plaintext Attack

As already mentioned in the introduction, there are a dozen of database encryption systems and schemes proposed in different communities. Nevertheless, adversary models that capture the query log security have never been defined or proposed before. As a venue for future work, the conclusions in this paper can be easily used to analyze the query log security for any existing or upcoming database encryption system or scheme.

References

1. Agrawal, R., Kiernan, J., Srikant, R., Xu, Y.: Order preserving encryption for numeric data. In: SIGMOD, pp. 563–574 (2004)
2. Arasu, A., Blanas, S.: Orthogonal security with cipherbase. In: CIDR (2013)

3. Bajaj, S., Sion, R.: TrustedDB: a trusted hardware based database with privacy and data confidentiality. In: SIGMOD, pp. 205–216 (2011)
4. Boldyreva, A., Chenette, N., Lee, Y., O'Neill, A.: Order-preserving symmetric encryption. In: Joux, A. (ed.) EUROCRYPT 2009. LNCS, vol. 5479, pp. 224–241. Springer, Heidelberg (2009)
5. Boldyreva, A., Chenette, N., O'Neill, A.: Order-preserving encryption revisited: improved security analysis and alternative solutions. In: Rogaway, P. (ed.) CRYPTO 2011. LNCS, vol. 6841, pp. 578–595. Springer, Heidelberg (2011)
6. Damiani, E., De Capitani Vimercati, S., Jajodia, S., Paraboschi, S., Samarati, P.: Balancing confidentiality and efficiency in untrusted relational DBMSs. In: CCS, pp. 93–102 (2003)
7. Hacigümüş, H., Iyer, B., Li, C., Mehrotra, S.: Executing SQL over encrypted data in the database-service-provider model. In: SIGMOD, pp. 216–227 (2002)
8. Hildenbrand, S., Kossmann, D., Sanamrad, T., Binnig, C., Faerber, F., Woehler, J.: Query processing on encrypted data in the cloud. Technical report 735, Department of Computer Science, Swiss Federal Institute of Technology Zurich (2011)
9. Katz, J., Lindell, Y.: Introduction to Modern Cryptography. CRC Press, Boca Raton (2008)
10. Popa, R., Redfield, C., Zeldovich, N., Balakrishnan, H.: CryptDB: protecting confidentiality with encrypted query processing. In: SOSP, pp. 85–100 (2011)
11. Rivest, R., Adleman, L., Dertouzos, M.: On data banks and privacy homomorphisms. In: DeMillo, R.A., et al. (eds.) Foundations of Secure Computation, pp. 169–178. Academic Press, New York (1978)
12. Sanamrad, T., Braun, L., Kossmann, D., Ramarathnam, V.: POP: a new encryption scheme for dynamic databases. Technical report 782, Department of Computer Science, Swiss Federal Institute of Technology Zurich (2013)
13. Sion, R.: Secure data outsourcing. In: VLDB, pp. 1431–1432 (2007)
14. Tu, S., Kaashoek, M., Madden, S., Zeldovich, N.: Processing analytical queries over encrypted data. In: VLDB, pp. 289–300 (2013)

A Multi-Party Protocol for Privacy-Preserving Range Queries

Maryam Sepehri[✉], Stelvio Cimato, and Ernesto Damiani

Dipartimento di Informatica, Università degli Studi di Milano, Crema, Italy
{maryam.sepehri,stelvio.cimato,ernesto.damiani}@unimi.it

Abstract. *Privacy-preserving query processing* (PPQP) techniques are increasingly important in collaborative scenarios, where users need to execute queries on large amount of data shared among different parties who do not want to disclose private data to the others. In many cases, *secure multi-party computation* (SMC) protocols can be applied, but the resulting solutions are known to suffer from high computation and communication costs. In this paper, we describe a scalable protocol for performing queries in distributed data while respecting the data owners' privacy. Our solution is applicable both to equality and range queries, and relies on a bucketization technique in order to reduce time complexity. We show the effectiveness of our approach through theoretical and practical analysis.

Keywords: Secure multi-party computation · Range query · Privacy-preserving query processing and bucketization

1 Introduction

Nowadays, large amounts of data are made available and shared in collaborative scenarios, where multiple data owners put together the information they have on the purpose of making accurate analysis and knowledge extraction. When data privacy is a concern, however, data owners are not willing to share plain text data with other parties. This is the case when legal constraints apply to the shared data (as for example data belonging to patients in hospital databases) or parties are at the same time competitor for commercial of financial reasons (as for example bank databases or list of customers from different competing companies).

Many techniques for *Privacy-preserving query processing* (PPQP) have been developed allowing data owners to respect data privacy when collaborating during the execution of queries. Such techniques are usually based on the application of *secure multi-party computation* (SMC) protocols. When the size of partitioned data is large, however, efficiency becomes a primary concern. Recently, different solutions for privacy-preserving queries in SMC paradigm have been proposed [1–7]. For instance, privacy preserving set intersection [2–5], which enables computing items common to private databases in a privacy-preserving way, is a fundamental operation for performing equality test query [8,9], i.e. selecting items

W. Jonker and M. Petković (Eds.): SDM 2013, LNCS 8425, pp. 108–120, 2014.
DOI: 10.1007/978-3-319-06811-4_15, © Springer International Publishing Switzerland 2014

in a database that are equal to a given value fall in a given range [9–11]. Our own recent work includes a technique, the *B-SMEQ* (Bucketized Secure Multi-party protocol for Equality test Queries) [12] supporting efficient execution of equality test queries on shared data. In this paper, we propose an extension of our technique to execute privacy-preserving range queries over partitioned data in scalable manner.

Three categories of solutions have been proposed for privacy-preserving range queries: those based on a specialized data structure [10,11,13], those exploiting order-preserving encryption techniques [14,15], and those relying on bucketization approaches [8,16]. Regardless of the category, these solutions focus on the data outsourcing paradigm, i.e., when all the data are outsourced to a third party server, and do not handle scenarios in which different parties are jointly collaborating in query execution. The solution we present transforms a range query over real numeric data in a sequence of equality test queries, each resolved using B-SMEQ. The paper is organized as follows. In the next section some related work is discussed, while in Sect. 3 the problem of privacy-preserving range queries is introduced and some preliminary notions are discussed. In Sect. 4, we present secure range queries in multi-party paradigm. The privacy of our protocol is analyzed in Sect. 4.5. In Sect. 5, we summarize the results we have obtained by simulation. Section 6 describes our conclusions.

2   Related Work

Much research has been done on techniques for querying encrypted outsourced databases, and many techniques for performing equality and range queries over encrypted data have been developed [16–19]. Encryption techniques used for database outsourcing usually do not preserve order and therefore query predicates with comparison operators can not be straightforwardly evaluated on encrypted values. For this reason, authors in [14,15] proposed a solution based on the exploitation of order preserving encryption schemes for supporting range queries on encrypted data, while others have put forward bucketization-based approaches [8,16] . However, these solutions have been tailored to the data outsourcing paradigm. To the best of our knowledge, no applicable solutions for the execution of privacy-preserving range queries in multi-party collaborative scenarios exist in the literature. In the remainder of this paper, we will show how the idea underlying equality test protocol proposed in [12] can be extended to tackle this problem, computing range queries respecting data privacy.

3   Preliminaries

In this section, we briefly go over some definitions that will be used to describe our approach: We describe first the basic scenario, the set intersection protocol on which our solution is based, and then the B-SMEQ technique [12].

3.1   Basic Scenario

In our setting, the multi-party system consists of the following components:

- A set of data owners $O = \{O_1, \ldots, O_m\}$, which are arranged into a logical ring.
- A collection of horizontally partitioned data $T = \{T_1, \ldots, T_m\}$ belonging to $\{O_1, \ldots, O_m\}$, respectively. Each table T_i may contain a set of searchable attributes $T_{i,A_1,\ldots,A_{g_1}}$ and extra attributes $T_{i,B_1,\ldots,B_{g_2}}$. In this paper, we assume $g_1 = g_2 = 1$ to simplify the protocol description.
- A group of authorized users[1] U enabled to execute query q over T.

Here, we suppose that data owners are *honest-but-curious* i.e., they honestly follow the protocol, but they are curious to learn as much as they can. Given a query q spanning over the partitioned data T by an authorized user, the aim is to obtain the answer to query q while satisfying the following properties:

data privacy: the user learns only the result of the query; *query privacy:* data owners do not learn the query; *query anonymous result:* the user does not know whom the results belong to.

3.2   Set Intersection Protocol

The set intersection protocol proposed by Agrawal et al. [4] relies on a commutative encryption scheme. Informally, a commutative encryption is a pair of encryption functions f and g such that $f(g(v)) = g(f(v))$. Thus by using the combination $f(g(v))$ to encrypt v, we can ensure that one data owner cannot compute the encryption of value without the help of other data owners. In the following, we provide a quick summary of Agrawal's Set Intersection Protocol:

Input. Two parties S(sender) and R(receiver) with set of values V_S, V_R and keys k_s, k_r, respectively.

Output. $V_S \cap V_R$

Step 1. Both S and R apply hash function h to their own values and encrypt the result with their secret keys, $f_{k_s}(h(V_S)$ and $f_{k_r}(h(V_R))$.

Step 2. Sites S and R exchange $f_{k_s}(h(V_S)$ and $f_{k_r}(h(V_R))$ after randomly reordering their values to prevent possible inference attacks.

Step 3. Site S encrypts each value of the set $f_{k_r}(h(V_R))$ with k_s to obtain $Z_R = f_{k_s}(f_{k_r}(h(V_R)))$ and sends back the pairs $(f_{k_r}(h(V_R)), Z_R)$ to R.

Step 4. Site R creates pairs (v, Z_R) by replacing $f_{k_r}(h(V_R))$ with the corresponding v, where $v \in V_R$.

Step 5. In order to determine $V_S \cap V_R$, site R selects all v for which $Z_R \in f_{k_r}(f_{k_s}(h(V_S)))$.

---

[1] User authentication is outside the scope of the current paper and will not be discussed here.

3.3   Bucketized-Secure Multi-party Equality Test Queries (B-SMEQ)

In this section, we summarize our bucketization-based solution for equality test problem, called B-SMEQ [12]. The scenario allows an authorized user u asks for all tuples in T whose searchable attribute is equal to searched value v. B-SMEQ relies on a bucketization technique on searchable attribute that allows each data owner, during the computation phase, to select the bucket corresponding to v, thus resulting in lower computation and communication costs.

The protocol includes two phases: Phase 1 is executed only once by a trusted third party (TTP) for the realization of the bucketization scheme, whereas phase 2 is executed each time a query is processed.

- Phase 1 (Computation Matrix W). Each data owner O_i separately computes a local permutation π_i of bucket indices vector $(1, 2, \ldots, s)$ and sends it to TTP, who in turn generates a random permutation π of $(1, \ldots, s)$ and an interchange matrix W based on $\pi_1, \ldots, \pi_m$. Details on the computation of matrix W can be found in [12].
- Phase 2 (Query protocol). In this phase Agrawal's Set Intersection Protocol is executed to to find the intersection among the query and the results collected by the owners. More in detail, to compute the result of the query, each data owner sends its data in encrypted form to the next participant. This way, each data owner holds the data of its predecessor in the ring. When a user u wants to submit an equality query looking for value v, u gets the bucket ID corresponding to v from TTP permutation π. Then the bucket ID is sent to the initiator[2], who selects the corresponding bucket from the predecessor's data, super-encrypts them with its own key and sends it to the next participant. The procedure is repeated for each data owner in the ring; the selected buckets are propagated along the ring until they have been encrypted using all owner's private keys. Once all data owners hold the buckets encrypted with all keys, the buckets, denoted by R_q, are sent to u along with the query q encrypted by all the owner's keys, denoted by $\bar{q} = E_{k1, k_2, \ldots, k_m}(E_u(q))$. The user, after decrypting $\bar{q}$ with her own key, obtains $\bar{\bar{q}} = E_{k1, k_2, \ldots, k_m}(q)$. Since the adopted encryption scheme is commutative, u can now match $\bar{\bar{q}}$ with the searchable attribute of R_q to find which tuples correspond to the original query q.

4   Range Query in Secure Multi-party Paradigm

In this section, we apply B-SMEQ to executing multi-party range query on numeric data. We present two protocols, the first designed to work for range queries on integers, and the second for range queries on real numbers, achieving a significant reduction in communication complexity. Here, we focus only on the query processing phase for these two protocols, since we assume that phase 1 of B-SMEQ protocol has already been executed and each data owner is holding

---

[2] The initiator is selected at the time of matrix W generation by TTP.

the vector W_i that can be used to correctly select the buckets containing the values falling in the range query. For instance, let us assume that data owners $\{O_1, O_2, \ldots, O_m\}$ have received row vectors $\{W_m, W_1, \ldots, W_{m-1}\}$ from matrix W, respectively[3]; the owner who has received W_1 is called initiator.

4.1   Protocol 1

Input. A multi-party system with the data owner O_2 as initiator; range vector $\mathbf{r} = (r_{min}, r_{max})$; user query values $V_\mathbf{r} = \{x \in N | r_{min} \leq x \leq r_{max}\}$
Output. The set of tuples $R = \{t \in T | t.A \in V_\mathbf{r}\}$.

Step 1. Both user u and data owner O_i apply the hash function h to their sets. Let $\bar{V}_r = h(V_\mathbf{r})$ be the result of hashing for the user and let $\bar{T}_{i,A} = h(T_{i,A})$, for each $i \in \{1, \ldots, m\}$, be the hashing of the set values $T_{i,A}$. Two randomly secret keys are selected, k_r for u and $\langle k_i, k_i' \rangle$ for data owner O_i.
Step 2. u encrypts $\bar{V}_r$ and sends $\bar{\bar{V}}_r = f_{k_r}(\bar{V}_r)$ to all data owners.
Step 3. Each data owner O_i, $1 \leq i \leq m$, does the following:
3.1 Computes $f_{k_i}(\bar{T}_{i,A}) = Y_i = \{y_i = f_{k_i}(x) | x \in \bar{T}_{i,A}\}$.
3.2 Generates a set of new keys, one for each value of attribute B, as $K_i^B = \{k_{ix} = f_{k_i'}(x) | x \in \bar{T}_{i,A}\}$.
3.3 Encrypts each value x in $T_{i,B}$ with the corresponding key k_{ix} to obtain $Y_i^B = \{E_{k_{ix}}(z) | z \in T_{i,B}\}$, where E is a symmetric encryption function.
3.4 Computes set $I_i = \{(v, f_{k_i'}(v)) | v \in \bar{V}_R\}$ for the purpose of decrypting the values of attribute B at user site. The data owner O_i randomly reorders the tuples Y_i and Y_i^B and sends them along with I_i to the next owner $O_{(i \bmod m)+1}$.
Step 4. u selects the set of buckets $B = \{i | 1 \leq i \leq s\}$ that contains values of $V_\mathbf{r}$, and sends $\bar{B} = \{\bar{\pi}_k | k \in B\}$ to O_2 as an initiator.
Step 5. At this step, each data owner O_i holds data Y_{i-1} of O_{i-1}. For every item j belonging to $\bar{B}$, O_2 sets $h_2 = W_{1j}$, selects $Y_1(h_2)$ i.e., the bucket in Y_1 where ID is h_2, and overencrypts with her own key. Then O_2 sends h_2 to the next owner. When data owner O_i receives h_{i-1} from O_{i-1}, she sets $h_i = W_{(i-1)h_{i-1}}$, selects the corresponding bucket $Y_{i-1}(h_i)$ and sends the position h_i to O_{i+1}. This step continues until each data owner selects the buckets corresponding to $V_\mathbf{r}$.
Step 6. Each data owner O_i, $1 \leq i \leq m$, forms a set of triples $\langle Y_i, Y_i^B, I_i \rangle$ of her selection from step 5 and sends to the next data owner $O_{(i \bmod m)+1}$.
Step 7. Data owner $O_{(i \bmod m)+1}$ encrypts only Y_i with the key $k_{(i \bmod m)+1}$ and sends the triples $\langle f_{k_{(i \bmod m)+1}}(Y_i), Y_i^B, I_i \rangle$ after reordering to the next participant in the ring. This process is repeated until Y_i is encrypted by all keys of m data owners, obtaining $Z_i = f_{k_1}(f_{k_2}(\ldots(f_{k_m}(Y_i))))$, up to a permutation of the encryption keys[4].

---

[3] Without loss of generality, the association of row vectors to data owners can be changed according to the selected permutation π_i when the TTP generates the matrix W.

[4] The keys $k_1, k_2, \ldots, k_m$ represent a commutative set of keys.

Step 8. Each data owner O_i sends $\langle Z_i, Y_i^B, I_i \rangle$ to O_2, who in turn passes the set $\bar{\bar{V}}_{\mathbf{r}}$ through the ring in order to have it encrypted by all keys $k_1, \ldots, k_m$ for obtaining $\tilde{V}_{\mathbf{r}} = f_{k_1}(\ldots(f_{k_m}(f_{k_r}(\bar{\bar{V}}_{\mathbf{r}}))))$, and then sends back $\hat{V}_r$ with the set of triples $\langle Z_i, Y_i^B, I_i \rangle$ to the user, for all $i \in \{1, \ldots, m\}$.

Step 9. User u decrypts each value $\tilde{v} \in \tilde{V}_{\mathbf{r}}$ with the own decryption key to obtain set $\hat{V}_{\mathbf{r}}$, and then for each i, $1 \leq i \leq m$:

- Finds tuples in Z_i whose entry related to attribute A is equal to jth value of $\hat{V}_{\mathbf{r}}$;
- Considers the entry corresponding to attribute B of those tuples;
- Decrypts the jth value of I_i with k_r, obtaining $f_{k_i}(\tilde{v})$;
- Uses $f_{k_i}(\tilde{v})$ to decrypt the corresponding entry in Y_i^B.

For instance, suppose that user u asks for tuples belonging to range $\mathbf{r} = [29, 42]$ w.r.t. attribute $T.A$. According to the proposed protocol, u sends an equality query for each integer value in

$$V_{\mathbf{r}} = \{29, 30, 31, 32, 33, 34, 35, 36, 37, 38, 39, 40, 41, 42\}$$

Then, each equality query is computed by using B-SMEQ protocol. While straightforward, this approach has two primary disadvantages: first, it has high computation and communication costs, and second, it has a limitation on domain type, since not all ordered domains can be handled this way; for instance, floating point values do not lead themselves well to this type of representation. To handle these problems, we split values of searchable attribute to improve the protocol.

4.2   Protocol 2

We are now ready to improve Protocol 1 to support range query over real searchable attribute by splitting each real number into two values. The aim of splitting real numbers is to provide a finite discrete domain in which range queries can be resolved by using Protocol 1. Accordingly, we introduce two main modifications, one in the pre-processing and the other in post-processing phase.

Pre-processing Phase

- *Data owners side*: Each data owner O_i splits the attribute $T.A$ into two sub attributes $T.X$, $T.Y$ as follows:
  - $\forall v \in T.A$, $v = v_x + v_y$
  - Suppose that $v_1 v_2 \ldots v_c$ is the integer part of v. Then we set $v_x = v_1.10^{c-1}$, $v_y = v - v_x$. Observe that $v_x \in N$ by definition and that T.Y is considered an extra attribute, only T.X is used as searchable attribute.
- *User side*: Suppose that q is a range query, with range $\mathbf{r} = (r_{min}, r_{max})$, the user u wants to perform.
  - User u splits range boundaries as described above, obtaining $r_{min} = r_{min,x} + r_{min,y}$, $r_{max} = r_{max,x} + r_{max,y}$

- Suppose that α is the most significant digit of $r_{min,x}$ and β is the most significant digit of $r_{max,x}$, and that c_1 and c_2 are the number of digits of $r_{min,x}$ and $r_{max,x}$ respectively.
- The range query q is mapped onto 3 categories of equality queries:
$$q^{(1)} := \{i.10^{c_1-1}, i \in \{\alpha, \alpha+1, \ldots, 9\}\}$$
$$q^{(2)} := \{\gamma.10^{\bar{c}}, \gamma \in \{1, 2, \ldots, 9\}, c_1 - 1 \prec \bar{c} \prec c_2 - 1, \bar{c} \in N\}$$
$$q^{(3)} := \{\eta.10^{c_2-1}, \eta \in \{1, 2, \ldots, \beta\}\}$$
- The query sets $q^{(1)}$, $q^{(2)}$, $q^{(3)}$ are computed then by adopting Protocol 1.
- Observe that for each range $[10^i, 10^{i+1}], i \geq 1$, in Protocol 2 we compute at most 10 equality queries, whether in Protocol 1 we compute $(10^{i+1} - 10^i)$ equality queries.

Post-processing Phase

- *User side.* Suppose that $S^{(1)}, S^{(2)}, S^{(3)}$ are the results obtained by the user for the equality set $q^{(1)}, q^{(2)}, q^{(3)}$, respectively. By definition of $q^{(2)}$, all the tuples in $S^{(2)}$ are in the range $\mathbf{r} = (r_{min}, r_{max})$. The user u should only select from $S^{(1)}$ those tuples t for which $t.y \geq r_{min,y}$, and from $S^{(3)}$ those tuples t such that $t.y \leq r_{max,y}$.

4.3   A Worked-Out Example

As an example, consider the ring of three data owners shown in Fig. 1(a), where each owner has a searchable attribute A on real numbers along with corresponding bucket number. According to the protocol description in Sect. 4.2, each data owner first splits every $v \in A$. For instance, data owner O_1 follows the pre-processing phase and obtains $v_x = 10$, $v_y = 7.7$ for $v = 17.7$ (Fig. 1(b)). Now, suppose that user u asks for tuples t whose searchable attribute value is within the range $\mathbf{r} = [8.62, 242.0]$. Then, u splits $r_{min} = 8.62$ and $r_{max} = 242.0$ to $r_{min,x} = 8$, $r_{min,y} = 0.62$ and $r_{max,x} = 200$, $r_{max,y} = 42.0$, respectively. By definition, u sets $\alpha = 8$, $\beta = 2$, $c_1 = 1$ and $c_2 = 3$ to obtain $q^{(1)} = \{8, 9\}$, $q^{(2)} = \{10, 20, \ldots, 90\}$ and $q^{(3)} = \{100, 200\}$. Then u sends the equality queries $q^{(1)}$, $q^{(2)}$ and $q^{(3)}$ to data owners, who in turn execute protocol 1 and return the corresponding results $S^{(1)}$, $S^{(2)}$ and $S^{(3)}$ to the user. Finally, a post-processing phase is required to weed out the false positives from $S^{(1)}$ and $S^{(3)}$. Thus, u selects tuples t from $S^{(1)}$ for which $t.y \geq 0.62$ and from $S^{(3)}$ those tuples t such that $t.y \leq 42.0$.

4.4   False Positive Analysis

In this section, we analyze the impact of the data distribution, query distribution and number of buckets on the number of false positives that user gets in the query result (i.e. the tuples not belonging to the query range). More specifically, we tested Protocol 2 for $m = 3$ data owners, respectively with $n1 = 50000$, $n2 = 60000$, $n3 = 70000$ tuples in their own tables T_1, T_2 and T_3. We repeated

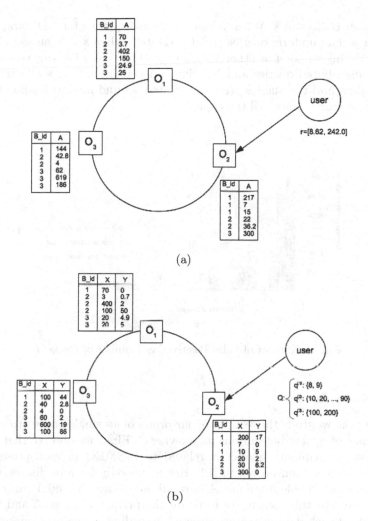

Fig. 1. (a) Three data owners with real searchable attribute A, (b) Each data owner splits attribute A into two sub attributes X and Y

the experiment with two data distributions: uniform distribution (UD) and normal distribution (ND) (mean $\mu = 50.5$, standard deviation $sd = 10$). Moreover, we also tried out two categories of queries, whose range was chosen respectively with a uniform and a normal distribution, with mean μ and standard deviation sd. Moreover, we repeated our experiment with $s = (5, 10, 15, 20, 25)$ number of buckets, computing exactly the same queries for each value of s. In Fig. 2, we show the results averaged across all the performed queries. Several remarks can be done based on Fig. 2. Firstly, the average number of false positives (FP) always decreases when s increases. This is more evident for uniform queries, for both UD and ND data. Furthermore, we observe that, with uniform queries, UD data has higher FP than ND data for $s = 5, 20, 25$, while it is almost the same for the other choices of s. When adopting normal queries for ND data, the FP is much less than uniform queries on UD/ND data when $s = 5$, almost the same when $= 10$, higher for the other values of s. This behavior suggests that for normally distributed queries and ND data bucketization is less effective, since both the data and the queries are concentrated around μ, thus leading to some buckets containing almost all the tuples.

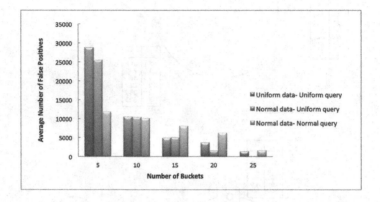

Fig. 2. Number of False Positives vs Number of Buckets

4.5 Privacy Issues

In this section, we study the security of our protocol for single query processing in the presence of honest-but-curious data owners[5]. First, we observe that privacy preservation for equality queries is related to B-SMEQ privacy preservation, which has already been proven in [12]. Hence, we only have to discuss whether splitting the searchable attribute A into sub attributes X and Y may lead to data leakage. For this reason, we focus on the privacy of Steps 5 and 7 where the records of each data owner are selected according to the user bucket ID.

– Step 5: Let us recall that at this step, each data owner holds the encrypted data of its predecessor in the ring .The only information that is visible to each data owner are bucket labels corresponding to tuples of its predecessor. Since the values of the predecessor are in encrypted form, there is no way in which the owner can find the relations between bucket ID and values of attributes X and Y. In this step, the owner selects the buckets corresponding to user query, which may reveal the size of buckets, but the owner does not know which bucket ID corresponds to the received tuples from the predecessor.

– Step 7: In this step each data owner receives the values of attribute X with different keys. However, since the values of attribute Y remained unchanged during the protocol execution, the data owner can infer the relationship between

---

[5] For now, we do not consider the case where a malicious participant can become aware of the distribution of query values by receiving multiple queries.

received set of X from different rounds. Nevertheless, there is no way in which the owner can access the actual values of the predecessor unless she is able to break the encryption.

According to the above informal analysis, our approach is secure in honest-but-curious model as long as no two data owners collude.

5   Time Complexity Analysis

In this section, we perform some experiments to clearly illustrate the benefit of bucketization approach for processing range queries in SMC paradigm in terms of communication time. We use Castalia[6] simulator on a Linux machine with dual Intel CPU running at 2.26 GHz, and 2 GB Ram. In the experiments, we construct 5 nodes in Castalia simulator including 3 data owners, 1 user and the TTP. Each data owner holds a table with one searchable attribute for range query where values are generated by sampling uniformly at random. To encrypt the searchable attribute of each data owner's table, we implemented a simple *commutative encryption* protocol based on *exponentiation modulo p*. For the range query, we prepared a set of 8 wide range queries Q, where the range predicates are defined on the selected attribute. Each query is selected randomly from uniform distribution.

We measured the communication time of our protocol for different number of buckets and different number of records, which are partitioned horizontally among 3 nodes. The experimental results are shown in Fig. 3. Each point in the figure corresponds to the average communication time obtained by running the query workload Q. The x axis shows the number of tuples N_i partitioned among data owners, where $N_i = 18.10^{i-1}$ for $1 \leq i \leq 5$. The y axis shows the average time of the query workload on the data owner side, which is dominated by the time of circulating buckets containing range values along the ring. The solid line of the plot displays the communication time of our protocol without using bucketization, whereas the dotted lines display the results of our protocol, which adopts bucketization on searchable attribute.

The dotted lines show the communication time when the searchable domain attribute $[1.0, 100.0]$ is divided into 5, 10 and 15 buckets having the same size. As Fig. 3 shows, the difference in communication time between solid and dotted lines increases fairly slowly when the number of tuples is relatively small, but it grows much faster as the number of tuples increases. The results confirm the fact that bucketization approach is effective in reducing the number of tuples circulating along the ring, resulting in lower communication time. Moreover, bucketization decreases communication time dramatically at first, for example when the number of buckets is 10, the protocol provides about 2 times improvement; however, then the marginal contribution of additional buckets to speed up tends to decrease. This behavior depends obviously on the domain of the searchable attribute, and does not depend on data and query distribution. We provide some examples in Sect. A of Appendix.

---

[6] http://www.omnetpp.org/component/content/article/8-news/3478

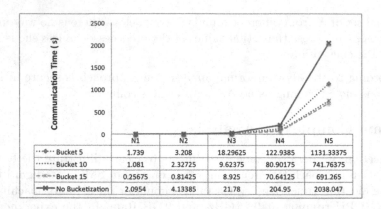

Fig. 3. Communication Time Comparison (Communication Time vs Number of Buckets)

6   Conclusions and Future Work

In this paper we extended our previous work to obtain a protocol for range queries in SMC paradigm. The proposed method exploits the relationship between range and equality queries to transform a range query in a set of equality queries. By appropriately splitting the searchable attribute, the number of equality queries is considerably reduced. Moreover, by adopting a bucketization technique which allows to work solely on a subset of data, our protocol scales well when large size data are considered. In our future work, we will extend our approach for supporting multidimensional range queries in a privacy-preserving way.

Acknowledgments. This work was partly supported by the EU project CUMULUS (contract n. FP7-318580).

Appendix

A   Finding Optimal Number of Buckets

For finding the optimal bucket number that is independent from the data and query distribution, we generate two different set of queries Q_{uni}, Q_{nor} in which each has 8 queries with wide ranges corresponding to the searchable attribute with range $[1.0, 100.0]$. Range of each query in Q_{uni}, Q_{nor} is selected randomly from uniform and normal distribution, respectively (Fig. 4).

For each experiment, we generated 4 range queries whose value is extracted according to a uniform distribution and 4 queries whose values are extracted according to a normal distribution on searchable attribute A with range $[1.0, \ldots, 100.0]^{7}$.

---

[7] For normal distribution, the standard deviation and mean are equal to $sd = 10$ and $\mu = 50.5$ respectively in order to ensure adequate coverage of buckets.

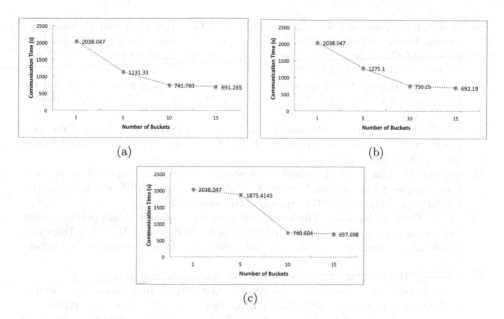

Fig. 4. (a) Uniform data-Uniform query, (b) Normal data-Uniform query and (c) Normal data-Normal query

References

1. Kerschbaum, F.: Outsourced private set intersection using homomorphic encryption. In: Proceedings of the 7th ACM Symposium on Information, Computer and Communications Security, ASIACCS '12, pp. 85–86. ACM, New York (2012)
2. Freedman, M.J., Nissim, K., Pinkas, B.: Efficient private matching and set intersection. In: Cachin, C., Camenisch, J.L. (eds.) EUROCRYPT 2004. LNCS, vol. 3027, pp. 1–19. Springer, Heidelberg (2004)
3. Kissner, L., Song, D.: Privacy-preserving set operations. In: Shoup, V. (ed.) CRYPTO 2005. LNCS, vol. 3621, pp. 241–257. Springer, Heidelberg (2005)
4. Agrawal, R., Evfimievski, A., Srikant, R.: Information sharing across private databases. In: Proceedings of the 2003 ACM SIGMOD International Conference on Management of Data, SIGMOD '03, pp. 86–97. ACM, New York (2003)
5. Vaidya, J., Clifton, C.: Secure set intersection cardinality with application to association rule mining. J. Comput. Secur. **13**, 593–622 (2005)
6. Yao, A.C.C.: How to generate and exchange secrets. In: Proceedings of the 27th Annual Symposium on Foundations of Computer Science, SFCS '86, pp. 162–167. IEEE Computer Society, Washington, DC (1986)
7. Goldreich, O., Micali, S., Wigderson, A.: How to play any mental game. In: Proceedings of the Nineteenth Annual ACM Symposium on Theory of Computing, STOC '87, pp. 218–229. ACM, New York (1987)
8. Hacigümüş, H., Iyer, B., Li, C., Mehrotra, S.: Executing sql over encrypted data in the database-service-provider model. In: Proceedings of the 2002 ACM SIGMOD International Conference on Management of Data, SIGMOD '02, pp. 216–227. ACM, New York (2002)

9. Damiani, E., Vimercati, S.D.C., Jajodia, S., Paraboschi, S., Samarati, P.: Balancing confidentiality and efficiency in untrusted relational dbmss. In: Proceedings of the 10th ACM Conference on Computer and Communications Security, CCS '03, pp. 93–102. ACM, New York (2003)

10. Boneh, D., Waters, B.: Conjunctive, subset and range queries on encrypted data. In: Vadhan, S.P. (ed.) TCC 2007. LNCS, vol. 4392, pp. 535–554. Springer, Heidelberg (2007)

11. Shi, E., Bethencourt, J., Hubert, T.-H., Dawn, C., Perrig, S.A.: Multi-dimension range query over encrypted data. In: IEEE Symposium on Security and Privacy, pp. 350–364. Smith (2007)

12. Sepehri, M., Cimato, S., Damiani, E.: A scalable multi-party protocol for privacy-preserving equality test. In: Franch, X., Soffer, P. (eds.) CAiSE Workshops 2013. LNBIP, vol. 148, pp. 466–477. Springer, Heidelberg (2013)

13. Li, J., Omiecinski, E.R.: Efficiency and security trade-off in supporting range queries on encrypted databases. In: Jajodia, S., Wijesekera, D. (eds.) Data and Applications Security 2005. LNCS, vol. 3654, pp. 69–83. Springer, Heidelberg (2005)

14. Agrawal, R., Kiernan, J., Srikant, R., Xu, Y.: Order preserving encryption for numeric data. In: Proceedings of the 2004 ACM SIGMOD International Conference on Management of Data, SIGMOD '04, pp. 563–574. ACM, New York (2004)

15. Boldyreva, A., Chenette, N., Lee, Y., O'Neill, A.: Order-preserving symmetric encryption. In: Joux, A. (ed.) EUROCRYPT 2009. LNCS, vol. 5479, pp. 224–241. Springer, Heidelberg (2009)

16. Hore, B., Mehrotra, S., Tsudik, G.: A privacy-preserving index for range queries. In: Proceedings of the Thirtieth International Conference on Very Large Data Bases, VLDB '04, vol. 30, pp. 720–731, VLDB Endowment (2004)

17. Song, D.X., Wagner, D., Perrig, A.: Practical techniques for searches on encrypted data. In: IEEE Symposium on Security and Privacy, pp. 44–55 (2000)

18. Goh, E.J.: Secure indexes. Cryptology ePrint Archive, Report 2003/216 (2003) http://eprint.iacr.org/2003/216/

19. Chang, Y.-C., Mitzenmacher, M.: Privacy preserving keyword searches on remote encrypted data. In: Ioannidis, J., Keromytis, A.D., Yung, M. (eds.) ACNS 2005. LNCS, vol. 3531, pp. 442–455. Springer, Heidelberg (2005)

Privacy Implications of Privacy Settings and Tagging in Facebook

Stan Damen and Nicola Zannone[✉]

Eindhoven University of Technology, Eindhoven, The Netherlands
s.damen@student.tue.nl, n.zannone@tue.nl

Abstract. Social networks are becoming increasingly popular nowadays. Users share personal information about themselves and other users in order to build and maintain their social network. However, the large amount of personal information available on social networks poses risks of data misuse. Although social networks offer users the possibility to specify privacy settings to regulate access to their information, these settings are often complicated and unintuitive, especially when dealing with new modalities of social communication like tagging. In this paper we investigate the privacy consequences of information sharing in social networks. In particular, we formally analyze the impact of the privacy settings and the use of tagging in Facebook on the visibility of information. To increase users' awareness of the risks of information sharing and empower users to control their information, we present a tool for determining the visibility of users' information based on their privacy settings and tagging.

1 Introduction

Online social network services, also called social networks, have become increasingly popular over the years. For instance, social networks like Facebook, Google+ and Twitter have millions of users across the world. The popularity of social networks is due to the fact that people want to keep in contact with their friends and meet people with common interests. Social networks provide a social environment in which users can share information with other users and build communities around common interests.

The most common way to share information is in the form of posts which can be placed by users on their own profile or on the profile of other users. Other examples include the possibility of sharing pictures, having profiles that are (partially) publicly available, and options to provide additional information about the user (e.g., location information). Many social networks also allow users to add to their profile (third party) applications which provide additional functionalities (e.g., games, online marketplaces, function enhancers) for sharing information and building their social network.

This work is funded by the Dutch national program COMMIT through the THeCS project.

W. Jonker and M. Petković (Eds.): SDM 2013, LNCS 8425, pp. 121–138, 2014.
DOI: 10.1007/978-3-319-06811-4_16, © Springer International Publishing Switzerland 2014

Social networks have also led to the introduction of new modalities of social communication for sharing information and building online communities. A prominent example of such new modalities is tagging which has been introduced by Facebook in 2009 [17]. Tagging allows users to share contextual information about themselves or their friends by linking a user to a certain content on the social network. In particular, a tag is a label specifying a user's name and provides a link to that user's profile.

From a user's viewpoint, the uncontrolled sharing of personal information poses potential privacy threats [18,23]. In particular, information available on social networks can be misused by other users (e.g., cyberstalking [11], identity theft [4,27] and discrimination [12]). In order to address user privacy concerns, many social networks allow users to specify privacy settings in order to regulate the visibility of their information. In addition, tools are available within social networks to help users visualize their social circle and the visibility of the information posted in their profile.

Although privacy settings provide users some control over their information, such settings are often complicated and unintuitive. In particular, they may mislead users by providing confidence to be in full control of their information. Many users believe they are solely sharing data with their friends and are unaware that the actual visibility may not reflect their privacy settings [32]. For instance, tags modify the visibility of objects, making it difficult for users to determine to what extent a piece of information is visible. Moreover, tools for viewing the user's profile from the perspective of other users often do not reflect the real visibility of information. As a consequence, they provide a false perception that leads users to underestimate the risks of sharing information.

Another main privacy issue concerns the user who is in control of the information. In social networks, the user in control of the information is usually the user who owns the profile in which the content is posted. In contrast, privacy regulations (e.g., Directive 95/46/EC and its subsequent regulation) empower the data subject – i.e., the user to whom the information refers – to control the processing and disclosure of his data [9].

To enable users to control the use of their data, we need collaborative access control systems able to support the functionalities provided by social networks. Moreover, these systems should increase users' awareness of the privacy risks of sharing information. In particular, they should assist users in ensuring that the specified settings reflect their intentions and in understanding the privacy consequences of sharing information.

This work takes a first step in the development of such systems. We formally analyze the impact of privacy settings and tagging on the visibility of information in Facebook and identify drawbacks in the privacy controls used to regulate access to information. First, we model user profiles in Facebook along with the objects that can be shared by users as well as the role of users with respect to information. We use the profile model to study how the visibility is determined by privacy settings and tagging. In particular, the model has been used to develop a proof-of-concept tool which aims to increase awareness and empower users to control their information. The tool implements Facebook's privacy controls in Prolog, and allows users to determine the visibility of their information based on their settings and tags. To make the discussion more concrete, we analyze a number of scenarios that are representative for real situations in Facebook.

The paper is organized as follows. Section 2 discusses the privacy issues in social networks. Section 3 presents the Facebook profile model, and Sect. 4 demonstrates the effect of privacy settings and tagging on the visibility of information using some examples. Section 5 presents an implementation of Facebook's privacy controls in Prolog to determine and analyze the visibility of information. Finally, Sect. 6 discusses related work, and Sect. 7 concludes the paper providing directions for future work.

2 Privacy Issues in Social Networks

To build and maintain their social circle, users of social networks are willing to share more and more information about themselves and about other users. Larcom and Elbirt [13] observe that *"the important common thread among these [social network] services is the exchange of personal information over the Internet"*. Thus, a huge amount of personal data is available on social networks nowadays. Although the sharing of personal data helps users build large social circles, this attitude poses privacy risks to them.

Several studies [10,15,18,23,25] have analyzed privacy concerns in social networks. Privacy issues in social networks can be classified into two categories.

Social network privacy practices: this category concerns privacy issues related to the collection and processing of personal data by the social network and their disclosure to third parties. Privacy issues in this category include user tracking (e.g., Facebook "Like" button [16]), user profiling for advertisement purposes and secondary usage of data [22], and storing information after it was deleted by the user.

Information disclosure to contacts: this category concerns privacy issues that arise from the misuse of personal information by other users in the social network. Privacy issues like cyberstalking [11], identity theft [4,27] and discrimination [12] fall under this category.

The first category is similar to the issues characterizing other domains in which personal data are handled by an organization. In this paper, we focus on the second category which is specific to social networks and, in general, to collaborative environments.

Users usually share their personal information on social networks voluntarily. Atwan and Lushing [2] observe that: *"There is only one thing in the world worse than being Facebook stalked, and that is not being Facebook stalked"*. This privacy paradox shows the contradictory desires of users: on the one hand, users want their privacy protected; on the other hand, they are willing to share more and more information about themselves in order to build and maintain their social network. Most users sacrifice their privacy in favor of their sociability. This choice is due to the fact that users are often not fully aware of the risks of sharing their information and of the widespread accessibility of information when posting on social networks.

Social networks allow users to specify privacy settings to control the visibility of the objects in their profile (i.e., who can see the object). This, however, may mislead users into believing they are in full control of their information. Even if users specify their privacy settings carefully, the information can be viewed by more users than the profile owner intended. For instance, in Facebook tagging a post modifies the visibility of the post. Moreover, by tagging a post or an image, a copy of the tagged post or image appears in the profile of the tagged user. The latter can then specify the visibility of the copy in his profile, regardless of the privacy settings of the original post.

The first intuition for analyzing the privacy issues in social networks and, in particular, the control over the information is that we need to distinguish the roles of users involved with the management of information. The profile owner has control of the information posted on his profile and in particular on its visibility. When posting on the profile of another user, a user retains some rights over the posted information. Tagged users have control over the tag and can influence the visibility of the information to which they are tagged. Last but not least, users can share information not only about themselves, but also about other users. Data subjects should be able to control the information about them and in particular its visibility. In the remainder of the paper, we refer to the problem of controlling the usage of information as the *multi-ownership* problem.

Multi-ownership introduces a number of privacy risks as it is not easy to understand to what extent users can control information, especially when users involved in the management of a piece of information specify conflicting privacy settings or are not aware of the privacy settings specified by the data host and of his relationship with other users. For instance, a user can establish a friend relationship with another user just to become close to a third user and therefore access the information in his profile without the latter knowing it. In addition, users may not be aware of the existence of content concerning themselves in the profiles of other users. The main issue here is that it is very difficult, if not impossible, to correctly identify the users to whom the information refers. Even if users would be aware, they have very little control over their information posted in the profile of other users. In particular, they have no authority to remove their information from other profiles or share it with a smaller group of users.

In this paper, we analyze the problem of multi-ownership and the issues introduced by the tagging functionality in Facebook. In particular, by formalizing the privacy settings in Facebook, we aim to study how tagging affects the multi-ownership problem and influences the visibility of information.

3   Facebook Profile Model

Facebook allows users to define privacy settings to control the usage of the information published in their profile (visibility, posting, removal, etc.). In the

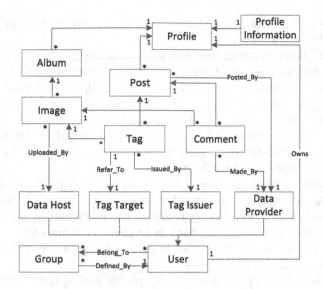

Fig. 1. Facebook Profile Model

remainder of the section, we describe the information contained in a Facebook profile and the permission that users have on such information. The Facebook profile model is presented in Fig. 1.

The main objects on Facebook are user profiles. Users can be individuals or organizations. A *profile* is created when a user signs up for the social network, and can be seen as a representation of the user. In particular, in Facebook a user is linked to a single profile and a profile to a single user. Therefore, we freely interchange the terms user and profile from here on. Every profile has a standard set of *profile information* associated with it (e.g., name, country, email address), and can contain one or more albums and posts. An *album* is a collection of *images*. A *post* is a message published in a profile. The main difference between images and posts is that images can only be uploaded on a user's own profile, while posts can also be placed on the profile of other users. Note that a user can post an image on the profile of another user; however, in this case the image is considered a post. Posts and images can have one or more comments and tags connected to it.[1] A *comment* is a note commenting a target object. A *tag* is a label that links a piece of information to a user profile. The concept of "wall", which is used on Facebook as a central place where content is visible, is not modeled since privacy settings cannot be defined at wall level.

We distinguish four roles that users can have in Facebook. The *data host* is the user that owns the profile in which the content is posted. The *data provider* is the user placing content on a profile in the form of posts, comments and images. The *tag issuer* is the user placing a tag on a post or an image. The *tag target* is

---

[1] Although Facebook also allows users to include tags in comments, we do not consider such tags in the paper as they do not change the visibility of objects.

the tagged user. Note that users can have more than one role on an object, e.g. data host and data provider.

To support users in organizing and managing their online relations, social networks employ the concept of *group*. A group consists of a set of users. Facebook provides users with a number of standard groups (i.e., friends, friends of friends, public, only me) as well as with the possibility to create custom groups specific to users' needs (e.g., school friends). Note that groups are specific to a profile, i.e., the membership of a user to a group should be determined with respect to the user who has defined the group. This is represented by cardinality "1 to many" for relation *defined_by* in Fig. 1.

The permissions that users can have on an object depend on their role on the object. The permissions supported by Facebook are "view", "delete", "post", "comment" and "tag". Note that permission to "comment" is implied by permission to "view"; permission to "tag" is implied by permission to "post" for posts and by permission to "view" for images. Therefore, we will not consider these permissions further in the paper.

The data host has all permissions on his profile and on the objects in it. The data provider can remove the content he posted at the condition he is in the current visibility of the object: if the data host changes his setting and the object is no longer visible to the data provider, then the data provider cannot remove the object anymore. Finally, the tag target has permissions to remove the tag from the content, regardless of its location. Facebook also supports the "control" permission, which represents the authorization to change profile settings. Such permission is always limited to the data host.

The permissions a user has on an object are also based on the visibility of objects. The visibility of an object is determined by its location, the privacy settings defined for the object and the tags associated to it. In Facebook, privacy settings can be specified at different levels of granularity, namely profile, profile information, album, post and image. The visibility of an object consists of the group defined by the data host in his settings for the object. Intuitively, a user can view the content in the profile of another user only if he belongs to the group to which the profile owner has granted permission to view the content. In addition, for every tag attached to a post, the same type of group, now defined by the tag target, is added to the visibility of the post. When a post or an image is tagged, a "copy" of the object appears on the profile of the tagged user. The visibility of the copy is determined regardless of the settings for the original object.

Facebook also allows users to specify profile settings. In this paper, we only consider the *post setting*, which specifies which group can post on the profile. The options for this setting are limited to friends or "no one" (i.e., only the profile owner can post). The other settings are used to specify default groups for the visibility of new objects. In addition, a user can specify whether the objects in which he is tagged should appear on his profile. In the remainder of the paper, we assume that this option is active with "friends" as visibility (note that these are the default settings in Facebook). This makes it possible to study information dissemination, of which the data host is unaware.

4   Application of Privacy Settings

In this section, we analyze the multi-ownership problem and the effect of tagging through a number of scenarios that are representative for real situations in Facebook.

4.1   Scenario 1

This scenario analyzes a situation in which tagging is not used. It includes three users: Alice, Bob and Eve. Alice and Bob are friends. The scenario is shown in Fig. 2a.

Scenario 1(a). Alice posts some content on Bob's profile. Accordingly, Bob is the data host; Alice is the data provider. Bob assigns visibility *friends of friends* to the post. He can delete the post; Alice can delete the post as long as she is in the visibility of the post.

Scenario 1(b). Eve wants to view the information posted on Bob's profile without the latter knowing it. To this end, Eve becomes a friend of Alice. As the post has visibility *friends of friends*, Eve can view the post and all comments in response to it.

This simple scenario shows that, when using the standard posting feature of Facebook to share information, the data host is in full control of the content in his profile. One may argue that Bob may not know that Eve can view the post in his profile. However, Bob can simply avoid it by specifying more restrictive privacy settings. For instance, he can change the visibility of the post to *friends* or *only me*.

4.2   Scenario 2

This scenario extends scenario 1 by considering the use of tagging. Here, Bob is friend of Alice and Eve. The scenario is shown in Fig. 2b.

Scenario 2(a). Alice posts some content about Bob on her profile and tags Bob. Accordingly, Alice is the data host and data provider; Bob is the tag target. The visibility of the post is set by Alice to *friends of friends*. Because of the tag, the visibility of the post also includes the *friends of friends* of Bob. In addition, a copy of the post appears on Bob's profile (Bob is the data host for the copy). The visibility of this copy is *friends* (of Bob) based on the default profile setting of Bob for tags. Because of the friendship relations between the users, Eve is part of the visibility of the post.

Scenario 2(b). Alice realizes Eve is in the visibility of the post and wants to stop sharing it with Eve while allowing her friends to view it. To do this, Alice changes the visibility to *friends*. As a consequence, the visibility of the post changes to Alice's *friends* and Bob's *friends*. Nonetheless, Eve remains part of the visibility, as she is Bob's friend.

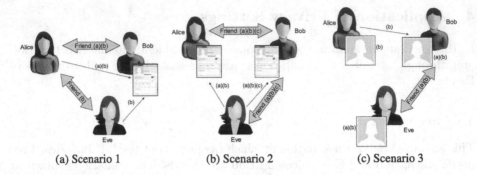

(a) Scenario 1   (b) Scenario 2   (c) Scenario 3

Fig. 2. Evaluation Scenarios

Scenario 2(c). Since changing the visibility to *friends* did not work, Alice changes the visibility to *only me* to prevent Eve to view the post. Thus, the visibility of the post changes to only Alice and Bob. However, Eve can still see the content in the post, as she can see the copy on Bob's profile.

This scenario illustrates the privacy risks caused by the extended, uncontrollable visibility induced by tagging. Alice changed the visibility in an attempt to remove a specific user from the visibility. However, due to the complexity introduced by the tag, even changing the visibility to *only me* does not have the desired result. The problem is that Alice depends on Bob for the visibility of the post. At this point, the only option left to Alice would be to remove the tag. However, by removing the tag Bob loses any form of control on the post, which is unacceptable from a privacy perspective as he is the subject of the content and therefore he should retain some authority on it. The alternative of leaving the tag attached to the post is also unacceptable, as Alice cannot restrict the visibility as desired. This simple example shows that the use of tagging in Facebook makes the multi-ownership problem, and control of the visibility, non-trivial.

4.3   Scenario 3

This scenario is based on scenarios 1 and 2, and aims to illustrate additional problems related to the use of tagging. Here, Bob and Eve are friends; Alice is not a friend of Bob and Eve. The scenario is shown in Fig. 2c.

Scenario 3(a). Bob uploads an embarrassing photo of Alice in an album that he shares with his friends. Bob tags Eve in the image, making an instance of the image appear on Eve's profile. The visibility of the image is Bob and Eve's *friends* (for the image in Bob's profile) and Eve's *friends* (for the image in Eve's profile). At this point, Alice may not be aware that a photo of her has been uploaded.

Scenario 3(b). A friend of Bob tags Alice to make sure everyone knows which person is the subject of the image.[2] Alice is notified that she has been tagged and, thus, she becomes aware of the existence of the image. In response, Alice deletes the image from her profile. However, the image still appears on Bob's profile, including the tag pointing to Alice. Alice decides to remove the tag as well. However, the image in Bob's profile and its copy in Eve's profile remain visible.

This scenario illustrates the lack of control users have over their information when posted on other users' profiles. Initially, Alice is not even aware that an image about her is posted (scenario 3(a)). She becomes aware in scenario 3(b) after she is tagged. However, she does not have the right to delete the image from other users' profile or even to restrict its visibility; she is only able to remove the image from her profile and the tag from the image.

4.4 Discussion

To analyze the consequence of information sharing, users require a good understanding of how the visibility of information is determined. However, privacy controls in Facebook are complicated and unintuitive. In particular, the scenarios above show that determining the visibility of objects becomes increasingly complex when tagging is used. For instance, tagging modifies the visibility of posts by including the tagged user's group corresponding to the one specified by the data host in his settings. As a consequence, users may share their information with more users than they intended.

Moreover, tags create a copy of tagged objects in the profile of the tag target. Facebook adopts an object-centric approach in which copies are treated as individual objects: users can define the visibility of copies in their profile regardless of the privacy settings for the original objects. This makes it difficult for the data host of the original object to restrict the visibility to certain users. For instance, scenario 2 shows that the only option Alice has to completely remove Eve from the visibility is to remove the tag.

To determine the actual visibility of the content (as opposed to objects) the data host of the original object needs to know the settings defined by the tagged user as well as his relations with other users. This, however, is impossible in Facebook as no one but the data host can visualize his settings. Although Facebook's choice of keeping settings private is reasonable, the settings for the original object should be considered when calculating the visibility of its copies.

The identification of data subjects and the control they have over their information are other crucial issues in social networks. Although tagging may be seen as a solution to the problem of linking a piece of information to the corresponding data subject, tagged users are not necessarily related to the information (see scenario 3). Indeed, the main goal of tagging in Facebook is to make information

---

[2] Bob's friend and Alice have to be friends as this is a requirement for tagging in Facebook.

easy to access rather than identifying the actual data subject(s). As a result, tagging can grant some control over the information to users that are not directly related to the information, increasing the risks of data misuse.

Even if data subjects are correctly tagged, they have limited control over their information (see scenario 3(b)). This is because Facebook assumes that the data host is the owner of the information. However, this is not always the desired solution. For instance, in scenario 3, it should be Alice in control of the visibility of the image; for Bob, delete permission would be sufficient. The obvious difficulty lies in determining the correct permissions for each piece of information, which is a non-trivial problem. However, making the data host automatically the owner is not a viable solution in all cases.

Another issue related to tagging is that when a user is tagged, the object automatically appears in her profile. The user may prevent it to occur by modifying the profile settings; however, this is a "one-size fit all" solution: either all contents in which she is tagged appear on her profile or none. A more desirable solution would be to let the tagged user pre-approve content before it appears on her profile.

5   Visibility Visualization Tool

In this section, we present an implementation of Facebook's privacy controls in Prolog for determining the visibility of users' information based on their privacy settings and tagging (available at http://security1.win.tue.nl/THeCS/). This proof-of-concept tool aims to increase awareness of the risks of information sharing and empower users to control their information.

5.1   Formal Representation of Privacy Settings

We use Prolog [1] to model and reason on the visibility of information based on user settings and tagging. First, we recap the Prolog concepts that are relevant to this paper.

An *atom* is an object of the form $p(t_1, \ldots, t_n)$ where p is an n-ary predicate symbol and $t_1, \ldots, t_n$ are terms (i.e., variables and constants). An atom is *ground* if $t_1, \ldots, t_n$ are constants. A *rule* is a construct of the form H :- $B_1, \ldots, B_n$ (with $n \geq 0$), where H is an atom called *head* and $B_1, \ldots, B_n$ (called *body*) are atoms. Intuitively, H is true if $B_1, \ldots, B_n$ are true. A *fact* is a rule with empty body (i.e., $n = 0$). A *program* is a finite set of rules.

Table 1 shows the predicates used to represent settings and objects in the Facebook profile and to reason about them. Predicates profile, profile-info, album, image, post, comment and tag are used respectively to identify profiles, profile information, albums, images, posts, comments, and tags. The first argument of these predicates is the ID of the object and is used to identify the object itself. In addition, objects are linked to a higher level object; the highest level object is the profile. Profile information, albums and posts are linked to a profile, images to an album, and comments to a post or an image. Intuitively, this link is used

Table 1. Predicates

Objects:
profile($profileID$)
profile-info($attributeID, profileID$)
album($albumID, profileID$)
image($imageID, albumID, tag\text{-}list$)
post($postID, profileID, poster, tag\text{-}list$)
comment($commentID, locationID, commenter$)
tag($tagID, issuer, target$)
Visibility:
setting($objectID, group$)
visibility-tag($objectID, visibility\text{-}list, tag\text{-}list$)
visibility($objectID, visibility\text{-}list$)
profile-setting($profileID, group$)
Membership:
friends($profileID_1, profileID_2$)
friendsOfFriends($profileID_1, profileID_2$)
belongsTo($profileID_1, (profileID_2, group)$)
member($profileID, visibility\text{-}list$)
Authorization:
can($profileID, permission, objectID$)

to identify the user/profile hosting the object. Predicates post, comment and tag specify the data provider (e.g., poster, commenter) or tag issuer. Predicates post and image specify the list of tags associated to them. Finally, tag specifies the user that has been tagged.

To determine the visibility of an object, we employ three predicates: setting for representing the privacy settings defined by the data host for the object, visibility-tag for tag induced visibility, and visibility for representing the object's visibility based on settings and tags. Predicate setting is a binary predicate where the first argument is an object ID and the second is the group specified by the data host as privacy setting (e.g., friends, public). Predicate visibility is a binary predicate where the first argument is an object ID and the second is a visibility list. A visibility list is a list of pairs ($profileID, group$); each pair specifies a group which is part of the object's visibility together with the user who defined the group. For example, the list $[(profile_1, friends), (profile_2, fof)]$ means that the friends of $profile_1$ and friends of friends of $profile_2$ form the object's visibility. The ternary predicate visibility-tag is similar to visibility; besides specifying the object ID and the visibility list of the object, it also provides the list of tags to be considered for determining the visibility of the object. In addition, we use the binary predicate profile-setting to specify post settings. The first argument is a profile ID, and the second denotes the group of users that can post on the profile.

The membership of a user to a group is determined using four predicates. Predicate member is used to determine whether a user is a member of the

Table 2. Rules for visibility, membership, and authorization

Visibility
1 visibility(ID, X) :- comment$(ID, LocationID, \_)$, visibility$(LocationID, X)$.
2 visibility$(ID, [(ProfileID, X)|Y])$:- post$(ID, ProfileID, \_, T)$, setting(ID, X), visibility-tag(ID, Y, T).
3 visibility-tag$(\_, [], [])$.
4 visibility-tag$(ID, [(X, Z)|Y], [TagID|T])$:- visibility-tag(ID, Y, T), tag$(TagID, \_, X)$, setting(ID, Z).

Membership
5 friends(X, X) :- profile(X).
6 friends(X, Y) :- friends(Y, X).
7 friendsOfFriends(X, Z) :- friends(X, Y), friends(Y, Z).
8 belongsTo$(X, (Y, friends))$:- friends(X, Y).
9 belongsTo$(X, (Y, fof))$:- friendsOfFriends(X, Y).
10 belongsTo$(X, (Y, public))$:- profile(X), profile(Y).
11 member$(S, [(X, Y)|Z])$:- belongsTo$(S, (X, Y))$.
12 member$(S, [T|Z])$:- member(S, Z).

Authorization
13 can$(S, delete, ID)$:- post$(ID, S, \_, \_)$.
14 can$(S, delete, ID)$:- comment$(ID, LocationID, \_)$, post$(LocationID, S, \_, \_)$.
15 can$(S, delete, ID)$:- tag$(ID, LocationID, \_)$, post$(LocationID, S, \_, T)$, in(ID, T).
16 can$(S, delete, ID)$:- post$(ID, \_, S, \_)$, visibility(ID, X), member(S, X).
17 can$(S, delete, ID)$:- comment$(ID, \_, S)$, visibility(ID, X), member(S, X).
18 can$(S, delete, ID)$:- tag$(ID, \_, S)$.
19 can$(S, view, ID)$:- visibility(ID, X), member(S, X).
20 can$(S, post, ID)$:- profile-setting(ID, X), member(S, X).

Copy Inference
21 copy$(ProfileID, PostID)$:- post$(PostID, \_, \_, Tags)$, tag$(TagID, \_, ProfileID)$, in$(TagID, Tags)$.

visibility list associated to an object. Predicate belongsTo is used to determine whether the user corresponding to $profileID_1$ is part of *group* as defined by the user corresponding to $profileID_2$ (Remark that groups are defined with respect to users). Predicate friends$(profileID_1, profileID_2)$ holds if the user corresponding to $profileID_1$ is a friend of the user corresponding to $profileID_2$. Similarly, friendsOfFriends$(profileID_1, profileID_2)$ holds if the user corresponding to $profileID_1$ is a friend of a friend of the user corresponding to $profileID_2$. Finally, predicate can is used to determine whether a user has a given permission (i.e., *view*, *post* and *delete*) on an object. Intuitively, can$(profileID, permission, objectID)$ holds if the user corresponding to $profileID$ can exercise *permission* on the object corresponding to $objectID$.

Table 2 provides the set of rules used to determine which permissions users have on a certain object. According to Prolog convention, we use symbol underscore (_) to denote an anonymous variable; intuitively, it means "any term".

Rules 1 to 4 determine the visibility of posts and comments.[3] The visibility of comments depends on the visibility of the post to which a comment belongs. Accordingly, rule 1 associates to a comment the visibility list of the post to which the comment belongs. Rule 2 determines the visibility list of a post based on its privacy settings and the list of tags associated to it. The visibility list of the post implied by the tags associated to it is recursively built using rules 3 and 4. In particular, rule 4 sets the visibility of the post to the same group specified by the data host in her setting, but now defined by the tag target.

Rules 5 to 12 are used to determine the membership of a user to a group. In Facebook the friendship relation is both reflexive and symmetric. These properties are represented by rules 5 and 6, respectively. Rule 7 uses predicate friends to determine the friends of friends of a user. Rules 8, 9, and 10 determine the membership of a user to groups *friends*, friends of friends (*fof*), and *public*. The membership of a user to group *only me* as well as to custom groups can be explicitly specified using predicate belongsTo. Rule 8 states that a user belongs to the group *friends* of a certain profile if he is a friend of the user of that profile. Rule 9 is analogous to rule 8 but for group *fof*. Rule 10 states that, if a profile exists, then all existing profiles are part of group *public*. Rules 11 and 12 recursively verify whether a user is in the visibility list of an object.

Rules 13 to 20 are used to determine the permissions that a user has on an object. A user has *deletion* rights over a certain object in three cases. Rules 13 to 15 state that the data host has the right to delete the objects in his profile (e.g., posts, comments, and tags). Predicate in is used to determine if a tag is one of the tags contained in the post. Rules 16 and 17 state that a user can delete the posts and comments he gave only if he is still within the visibility of the post and comment, respectively. Finally, a user can delete the tags that point to him (rule 18). Note that the tag issuer cannot remove the tags he created. He can only delete the tag by deleting the post that contains it.[4] Finally, a user has the permission to view an object if he is in the visibility of the object (rule 19). The permission to post is determined by checking the profile setting for posting (rule 20).

To determine the visibility of a certain content it is not sufficient to determine the visibility of the object in which the content is posted; we also need to determine the visibility of the copies of the object due to tagging. This can be done by adding rules that, given a set of tags, infer the copies of the tagged object. Rule 21 shows how the copies can be inferred using the original post and the tags associated to it. Then, the visibility of the content contained in a post can be determined as the union of the visibility of the post and the visibility of its copies. This choice reflects the fact that Facebook treats copies as separated objects on which the corresponding data host specifies his settings. Note that

---

[3] The rules for images and albums are similar to the ones for posts.

[4] A tag can be inserted in a post only when the post is created. Accordingly, the tag issuer and data provider coincide for posts.

deleting a copy can be done in two ways: either the user hosting the copy (i.e., the tag target) deletes it from her profile, or the data host or tag target removes the tag.

5.2 Proof-of-Concept

Facebook provides a functionality called "view as", which enables a user to look at her profile from the perspective of another user. In particular, using this functionality a user can determine the visibility of data objects in her profile from the perspective of a friend or a "public" user. However, this functionality only provides a partial view of the visibility. For instance, in scenario 1, Bob cannot verify whether Eve is in the visibility of the post. He can only verify the visibility that a public user has (Eve is not a friend of Bob), which shows that public users cannot view the information although Eve can. Moreover, the functionality does not consider tags to determine the overall visibility. In particular, the extended visibility introduced by adding tags to objects, as in scenario 2, is not shown; also copies of data objects are not considered for the visibility.

In contrast, the formalization of the Facebook profile model and privacy controls in Sect. 5.1 provides a visualization of the visibility which reflects the actual Facebook privacy controls. In particular, the proof-of-concept can accurately determine the visibility in situations involving tags and copies, like the scenarios in Sect. 4. A user can gain a more realistic insight into the access that others have to her information and therefore into the risks of information sharing by determining the visibility of her information, including instances of the information in other profiles. Based on this view, the user can choose to adapt her privacy settings, request removal of the information or report abuse to the social network.

To determine the visibility of a piece of information, it is necessary to consider all the users that should be involved in the management of that information, including the data subject(s). Tagging seems to be a viable solution for the identification of data subjects. Few approaches have been proposed to assist users in tagging images by identifying the subjects in an image. For instance, Stone et al. [24] propose a method for autotagging images within social networks which increases recognition performance beyond that of a baseline face recognition system. Facebook also provides an "autotagging" mechanism that automatically suggests possible tags for images. However, these tags often remain suggestions; moreover, they are only given to the data host who may not have incentive to accept them. In contrast, these tags should also be suggested to the data subject who can check the image and "accept" the tag. This approach has the added benefit of increasing data subject awareness which is a crucial step in improving user privacy in social networks.

To generate the complete visibility of a piece of information, the application would need access to the privacy settings of all involved users. However, in Facebook users can only access the settings of their own profile. Therefore, the proof-of-concept proposed in this paper cannot be deployed as a third party application.

It should be provided by Facebook as a functionality of the social network (which has the necessary administrative rights) like the "view as" functionality.

6   Related Work

Privacy in social networks has been extensively researched [7,8,19,30]. Many research efforts have been devoted to the design and analysis of privacy enhancing systems for social networks [14,20,31]. However, to the best of our knowledge, the impact of tagging on privacy and its relation with the multi-ownership problem have not been studied.

Several research efforts focus on the design of new privacy-friendly social networking sites. This is because existing social networks are often proprietary, and so it is difficult to validate the proposed approach. For instance, Cutillo and Mulvo [6] develop Safebook, a social network that handles privacy by real-life trust relationships. Baden et al. [3] propose Persona, a social network that uses user-defined privacy and attribute-based encryption. One attempt to enhance the privacy of existing social networks is Lockr [29]. Lockr is an access control system in which the social networking content is decoupled from functionality of social networks sites. This effectively removes the link between the user and the information and therefore enhances the control users have over their information. Differently from [29], the goal of this paper is to study the visibility of information in existing social networks rather than enhancing their privacy controls. In particular, our work is complementary to [29]: by having a complete view of the visibility of their information, users can effectively evaluate the consequences of sharing information and use existing techniques to restrict the access to it.

Another stream of research for enhancing privacy in social networks focuses on methods for controlled sharing of information. Controlled sharing among multiple users is often studied in the area of collaborative access control. Collaborative access control aims to balance the competing goals of collaboration and security [28]: collaborative systems aim to facilitate the sharing of information, while security aims to protect the same information. Tolone et al. [28] identifies the access control requirements for collaborative systems and analyzed existing authorization mechanisms with respect to such requirements. Although the identified requirements are general and applicable to social networks, they do not consider the new modalities of social communication that are emerging within social networks. Shen and Dewan [21] propose an access control model for collaborative editing. The model provides users a multi-dimensional, inheritance-based scheme for specifying access rights. Thomas [26] proposes team-based access control as an approach to applying role-based access control in collaborative environments. Yet, these models do not consider the new modalities of social communication. In addition, they mainly focus on organizational environments rather than on social networks.

In the context of social networks, a simple solution to the multi-ownership problem is proposed by Thomas et al. [25], in which the visibility of information is determined as the intersection of the privacy preferences of all involved users.

This method, however, may result in the unavailability of information when, for instance, two or more users restrict the visibility to "only me". Maximilien et al. [18] propose a privacy enhancing technology for evaluating profile privacy based on risk scores. Risk scores represent the level of privacy of a profile based on a comparison with other profiles and their respective settings. Recommendations are then made to lower the risk score based on the settings of other profiles. Another approach to collaborative access control in social networks is proposed in [23]. This approach maps user privacy specifications to an auction based on the Clarke-Tax mechanism [5] in order to select privacy policies that maximize social utility. In particular, privacy settings for an object are determined by a collaborative decision between the involved parties. However, this approach requires the data host to identify all involved parties and provides no proper incentive to do so.

7   Conclusions

Social networks are offering their users new modalities of social communication for sharing information and building social relations. These new modalities, however, introduce new privacy issues. In this work we have investigated the impact of privacy settings and tagging on the visibility of information in Facebook. The analysis of scenarios representative for real situations has shown that privacy controls in Facebook are unintuitive. In particular, they may provide users a false confidence of being in full control of their information and therefore they may lead users to underestimate the risks of information sharing. To increase awareness and enable users to control the access to their information, we implemented Facebook's privacy controls to determine the actual visibility of information also in presence of tags. The main characteristic of the proof-of-concept tool is that it is information-centric (as opposite to object-centric) in the sense that visibility is determined by considering all the occurrences of a piece of information.

The work presented in this paper suggests some interesting directions for future work. The proposed tool implements Facebook's privacy controls as they are. Such controls, however, suffer from a number of drawbacks; e.g., their enforcement is not transparent for the user and do not consider the data subject as a main actor in the decision making process. Existing work on collaborative information sharing does not fully solve the privacy problems in social network. Indeed, most approaches do not consider the various functionalities like tagging available nowadays in social networks, leaving out crucial information about content visibility. We argue that new approaches for collaborative information sharing on social networks are needed. Such approaches should support the full range of functionalities for information sharing offered by social networks. Moreover, they should make users aware of the consequence of privacy controls they define and the risks of sharing information. For instance, they should provide transparent conflict detection mechanisms that assist users in the identification and resolution of conflicts with the privacy settings of other users. Social networks will therefore need tools that assure that data are accessed according to the user's settings, or notify the user why the settings of other users have been assigned a higher priority.

References

1. Apt, K.R.: Introduction to logic programming. In: van Leeuwen, J. (ed.) The Handbook of Theoretical Computer Science, pp. 495–574. North Holland, Amsterdam (1990)
2. Atwan, G., Lushing, E.: The Facebook Book. Abrams Image, New York (2008)
3. Baden, R., Bender, A., Spring, N., Bhattacharjee, B., Starin, D.: Persona: an online social network with user-defined privacy. SIGCOMM Comp. Commun. Rev. **39**(4), 135–146 (2009)
4. Bilge, L., Strufe, T., Balzarotti, D., Kirda, E.: All your contacts are belong to us: automated identity theft attacks on social networks. In: Proceedings of WWW, pp. 551–560. ACM (2009)
5. Clarke, E.H.: Multipart pricing of public goods. Public Choice **11**, 17–33 (1971)
6. Cutillo, L.A., Molva, R., Önen, M.: Safebook: a privacy preserving online social network leveraging on real-life trust. IEEE Commun. Mag. **47**, 94–101 (2009)
7. Faliagka, E., Tsakalidis, A., Vaikousi, D.: Teenagers' use of social network websites and privacy concerns: a survey. In: Proceedings of PCI, pp. 207–211. IEEE (2011)
8. Gross, R., Acquisti, A.: Information revelation and privacy in online social networks. In: Proceedings of Workshop on Privacy In the Electronic Society, pp. 71 80. ACM (2005)
9. Guarda, P., Zannone, N.: Towards the development of privacy-aware systems. Inf. Softw. Technol. **51**(2), 337–350 (2009)
10. Gürses, S.F., Rizk, R., Gunther, O.: Privacy design in online social networks: learning from privacy breaches and community feedback. In: Proceedings of International Conference on Information Systems, Association for Information Systems, pp. 90 (2008)
11. Haron, H., Yusof, F.: Cyber stalking: the social impact of social networking technology. In: Proceedings of International Conference on Education and Management Technology, pp. 237–241. IEEE (2010)
12. Johnson, C.Y.: Project 'Gaydar' At MIT, an experiment identifies which students are gay, raising new questions about online privacy. Boston Globe (2009)
13. Larcom, G., Elbirt, A.: Gone phishing. IEEE Technol. Soc. Mag. **25**(3), 52–55 (2006)
14. Li, Q., Li, J., Wang, H., Ginjala, A.: Semantics-enhanced privacy recommendation for social networking sites. In: Proceedings of TrustCom, pp. 226–233. IEEE (2011)
15. Luo, W., Xie, Q., Hengartner, U.: FaceCloak: an architecture for user privacy on social networking sites. In: Proceedings of CSE, pp. 26–33. IEEE (2009)
16. Mack, E.: Facebook's 'Like' button illegal in German state. CNET news (2011)
17. Marlow, C., Naaman, M., Boyd, D., Davis, M.: HT06, tagging paper, taxonomy, Flickr, academic article, to read. In: Proceedings of the Seventeenth Conference on Hypertext and Hypermedia, pp. 31–40. ACM (2006)
18. Maximilien, E.M., Grandison, T., Liu, K., Sun, T., Richardson, D., Guo, S.: Enabling privacy as a fundamental construct for social networks. In: Proceedings of International Conference on Computational Science and Engineering, pp. 1015–1020. IEEE (2009)

19. Nagle, F., Singh, L.: Can friends be trusted? exploring privacy in online social networks. In: Proceedings of International Conference on Advances in Social Network Analysis and Mining, pp. 312–315. IEEE (2009)

20. Qing-jiang, K., Xiao-hao, W., Jun, Z.: The (P, α, K) anonymity model for privacy protection of personal information in the social networks. In: Proceedings of International Conference on Information Technology and Artificial Intelligence, pp. 420–423. IEEE (2011)

21. Shen, H., Dewan, P.: Access control for collaborative environments. In: Proceedings of Conference on Computer-Supported Cooperative Work, pp. 51–58. ACM (1992)

22. Spiekermann, S., Cranor, L.: Engineering privacy. TSE **35**(1), 67–82 (2009)

23. Squicciarini, A.C., Shehab, M., Wede, J.: Privacy policies for shared content in social network sites. VLDB J. **19**(6), 777–796 (2010)

24. Stone, Z., Zickler, T., Darrell, T.: Autotagging facebook: social network context improves photo annotation. In: Proceedings of Computer Vision and Pattern Recognition Workshops, pp. 1–8. IEEE (2008)

25. Thomas, K., Grier, C., Nicol, D.M.: unFriendly: multi-party privacy risks in social networks. In: Atallah, M.J., Hopper, N.J. (eds.) PETS 2010. LNCS, vol. 6205, pp. 236–252. Springer, Heidelberg (2010)

26. Thomas, R.K.: TeaM-based access control (TMAC): a primitive for applying role-based access controls in collaborative environments. In: Proceedings of Workshop on Role-Based Access Control, pp. 13–19. ACM (1997)

27. Thompson, H.H.: How I Stole Someone's Identity (Anatomy of a Social hack). Scientific American (2010)

28. Tolone, W., Ahn, G.J., Pai, T., Hong, S.P.: Access control in collaborative systems. ACM Comput. Surv. **37**(1), 29–41 (2005)

29. Tootoonchian, A., Saroiu, S., Wolman, A., Ganjali, Y.: Lockr: better privacy for social networks. In: Proceedings of International Conference on Emerging Networking EXperiments and Technologies, pp. 169–180. ACM (2009)

30. Young, A.L., Quan-Haase, A.: Information revelation and internet privacy concerns on social network sites: a case study of facebook. In: Proceedings of International Conference on Communities and Technologies, pp. 265–274. ACM (2009)

31. Yuksel, A.S., Yuksel, M.E., Zaim, A.H.: An approach for protecting privacy on social networks. In: Proceedings of International Conference on Systems and Networks Communications, pp. 154–159. IEEE (2010)

32. Zheleva, E., Getoor, L.: To join or not to join: the illusion of privacy in social networks with mixed public and private user profiles. In: Proceedings of WWW, pp. 531–540. ACM (2009)

Author Index

Printed in the United States
By Bookmasters

Printed in the United States
By Bookmasters